ROSE WINDOWS
for
QUILTERS

Rose window –

a circular window, especially one divided into compartments
by mullions radiating from a centre,
or filled with tracery suggestive of the form of a rose.
Also known as a catherine wheel or marigold window.

Shorter Oxford English Dictionary

ROSE WINDOWS
for
QUILTERS

Angela Besley

To my husband, who encouraged me from the beginning.

First published in 2000 by
Guild of Master Craftsman Publications Ltd,
166 High Street, Lewes, East Sussex BN7 1XU

Reprinted 2000, 2001

ISBN 1-86108-163-4

All photographs by Christine Richardson
Line drawings by Penny Brown, based on author's sketches

A catalogue record of this book is available from the British Library

Edited and designed by Margot Richardson

Typefaces: Caslon Open Face, Sabon, Gill Sans

Colour origination by Viscan Graphics Pte Ltd (Singapore)
Printed in China by Sun Fung Offset Binding Co., Ltd.

ACKNOWLEDGEMENTS

The author and publishers would like to thank Gail and Christopher Lawther for
their help and advice. Grateful thanks also to Persis Darling and Barbara Furse
for the items they made to include in this book.

CONTENTS

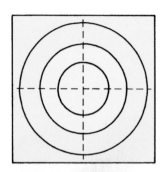

INTRODUCTION

Over the last few years I have been giving talks and workshops on rose-window quilts, and demonstrating the technique which I believe to be my own invention, at quilt fairs. There are always quilters who ask me when I am going to write a book on the subject – and now I have.

In about 1989 or 1990, *Good Housekeeping* magazine held a competition: to design a patchwork quilt, using at least four out of about ten specified Liberty fabrics. The first prize was to be a trip to New York on the *QE2*. As I was planning to visit New York in the near future, I decided to enter.

Unfortunately, I thought the fabrics were most unsuitable for patchwork. Instead of the pretty little prints which I had been using for my work, these were large prints in wild colours. I decided that the only possible thing to do with them was a design based on a stained glass window. Having a guide book to Chartres cathedral on my shelf, I glanced through it and settled on an adaptation of one of the great rose windows. The chosen design was painstakingly worked out, drawn onto graph paper with much help from my husband, and duly entered for the contest. It didn't even win one of the runner-up prizes!

I put the whole thing out of my mind for a long time, but eventually decided to make it as a wall hanging for my husband, as he had helped me so much with the design.

The following year I was in the USA attending a quilting summer school. The editors of *American Quilter* magazine saw my Chartres quilt which I had taken along for 'show and tell'. They asked me if they could use it on the cover of the magazine, where it appeared on the Winter 1992 issue.

All this time I had been teaching patchwork and quilting to members of a NATO community in Italy. Many of my students and friends, having seen 'The Quilt' hanging in my living room, started sending me postcards of rose windows which they had seen on their travels, and soon I decided to make more.

Above *The Art Nouveau Wall-Hanging by Barbara Furse is featured on pages 134–37.*

Left *This quilt, based on a rose window in St Eustache, Paris, was made by Persis Darling.*

Instructions for 'Sarah's Quilt', above, can be found on pages 94–97.

In the last year or so I have seen several rose-window quilts, both in Europe and in the USA, but I believe that my 'Chartres' quilt was the first one in which this technique was used.

I must stress that in my work I am not trying to reproduce the subject matter of the windows, which is often very complex and mystical, but I am trying to make something beautiful using shapes and colour.

I am now looking forward to sharing with you this fascinating way of having the colour and beauty of a rose window in your own home.

Equipment and Materials

You will need a basic sewing kit for all the projects in this book: that is, needles, pins, suitable sewing thread in an assortment of colours, tacking cotton, and scissors for cutting paper in addition to a pair for fabric.

Fabric This can be of any type, although I prefer to use cottons, on the whole, for any project which will need to be washed at some time. For such items as wall-hangings or framed pictures any materials can be used: silk, synthetics, wool, lamés (fabrics containing gold or silver threads), foil, plastics, etc. You will see that the sofa throw in this book (see page 116) is made with a selection of the exotic fabrics which my daughter, Gail Lawther, uses most of the time.

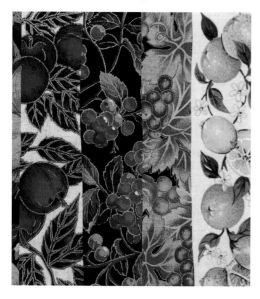

Fabrics can range from plain colours to bold repeating patterns, where segments of the repeat can be used to great dramatic effect.

Wadding and interfacing For most projects you will need wadding. Both cotton and polyester waddings are available from sewing and quilting suppliers. When I work on a dark background I usually use a dark wadding. I realised that this was a good idea when a wall-hanging which I had finished began to 'beard': that is, the wadding had begun to creep through the background fabric. At first I thought it was cat hairs (my cat loves quilts; cats and quilts seem to go together, somehow) and I tried to pick them off, with no success at all: they just seemed to get longer. Of course, these days wadding seldom beards, but I like to be sure. (One American company makes a charcoal grey wadding which is excellent.)

Heavy interfacing (such as Craft Vilene) is very useful, as it can be left in the finished article to give depth. In some cases, it can do away with the need for quilting.

Materials for quilting (left) include:

1 *Variety of fabrics*
2 *Heavy interfacing*
3 *Wadding*
4 *Thick (double-knit) wool for trapunto (see page 26)*
5 *Stranded embroidery thread for decorative stitching*
6 *Variety of threads for stitching and quilting*
7 *Iron-on black bias tape*

Thread This, course, is another necessity. You will need thread for appliqué, for quilting, for embroidery. I prefer to use cotton thread for appliqué, especially when I am using cotton fabric, as a synthetic thread will sometimes cut into the fabric. However, there are no rules about this. A cotton-wrapped polyester quilting thread is the best for quilting. As for embroidery threads, the sky's the limit as 'they' say. You can embellish your quilts by hand or machine with any of the wonderful threads available nowadays, and/or with beads, sequins and anything else you can think of.

Quilting pulls the three layers – background fabric, wadding and backing fabric – together, around the appliqué, which then appears to be three-dimensional.

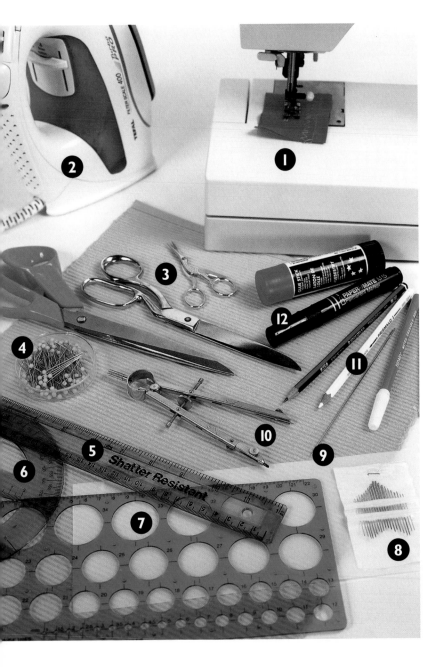

Drawing and marking You will also need pencils, a permanent marker, template plastic (available from quilting suppliers), protractor (the largest you can find or afford), chalk pencil or soapstone pencil (for marking dark fabrics), rulers and a pair of compasses. (At a workshop I attended in America, one student brought the type of compass used for direction-finding!)

Other useful tools are the plastic templates for drawing circles and ovals, to be found in stationers', art or office-supply shops. I have found these particularly helpful while making the projects for this book and needing to work faster than usual. Using them, you can draw circles and ovals directly onto card, interfacing or fabric, without the bother of first making a plastic template. You will probably find that you already have most of these things in your possession (or your husband or children can be persuaded to lend them).

So, get your tools and fabrics together – *and have fun!*

Tools for quilting (above) include:

1   Sewing machine
2   Iron
3   Variety of scissors for cutting fabric, paper, template plastic and thread
4   Glass-headed pins
5   Ruler

6   Protractor
7   Bought template for circles
8   Sewing needles
9   Trapunto needle (see page 26)
10 Pair of compasses
11 Chalk pencil for marking on dark fabrics
12 Marking pens for fabrics

Your Questions Answered

Here are some of the questions I am asked when I am demonstrating, and the answers I usually give.

What kind of fabric do you use?

I usually use cotton, as I love the crisp feel of it, but you can use any fabric.

Should I wash the fabric before I use it?

If I am making a wall-hanging I never wash the fabric as I like the slight stiffness of new fabric. On the other hand, if I am making an article which will be in constant use and will need washing, such as a cushion cover, a tablecloth or a bed quilt, then I wash and press it, so that when the finished item is washed the colours won't run and the article won't shrink.

Is this kind of work difficult?

It can be as easy or as difficult as you wish. Some shapes are really simple to work with and some are more difficult (see page 19). You will also see in some of the project instructions that there are ways of dealing with an awkward shape to make it easier to use.

Some of the shapes in the 'Washington' Wall-Hanging (page 102) are among the most involved in this book – but are not difficult to make, given a little practice.

Do you quilt all your work?

I would usually quilt a wall-hanging or a cushion cover but not a tablecloth, which would drape better without quilting. A framed picture might need quilting to give it some depth but it is not necessary if the applied pieces have some sort of interlining.

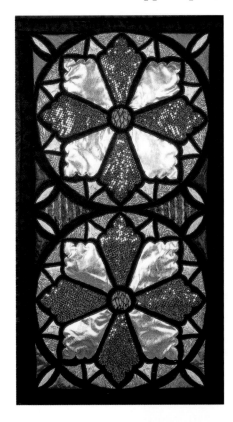

How should I choose which colours to use?

I can't tell you this, I'm afraid. Colour is a very personal thing: for instance, I don't like yellow and I have to force myself to use it now and again but I have friends who just love it.

Go with the colours you like, but if you really want your work to make an impact, use the brightest, or most dramatic colours you can find. If a fabric shouts at you from a stand at a quilt show or in a shop, buy it.

Think about the windows you have seen in the great churches and cathedrals: no one agonised over which colour went with what when those windows were created; they just wanted to make the most beautiful picture in glass.

I have included a few 'windows' in lighter and softer colours in this book to give plenty of variety, and to show how versatile the technique is, but I prefer the brighter colours.

The Monochrome Sofa Throw (above) employs texture and sheen to make a dramatic statement, while the 'Chartres' Wall-Hanging (half shown, right) uses bold patterns not normally found in traditional quilt-making.

How long did that piece take you?

Another impossible question to answer, as far as I am concerned. I often work on several pieces at once, and they are usually at different stages. I never count up how many hours I spend on one piece.

I was once making a bed quilt, and had been working on it for about three years, when it suddenly needed to be completed in a month, to go into a book my daughter was writing.

At the time, I was living in Italy. It was August, and the temperature was in the nineties. Of course, I said I could do it: she was going to pay me to do it, after all! I worked like a slave, most days sitting by a fan, wearing very little, with a scarf around my neck to catch the drips, but I finished it, and wrote the instructions, just in time for a friend who was flying home the next day to deliver it to my daughter at Gatwick Airport. Phew!

On the other hand, I have just made two wall-hangings entirely by hand in a month. It depends on how much time you can give to a project and how many other things you have to do. Fortunately, I am lucky enough to have a very supportive husband who encourages me in my work and doesn't complain about the dust-bunnies under the beds, and the occasional boring meal. I know that was a rather long-winded explanation, but I wanted to explain that, as in all things, you can do them if you really want to.

Making a simple 'kaleidoscope' greetings card (above) – which takes only a little time – can be just as satisfying as a complex quilted pattern, in this case a cushion cover (left).

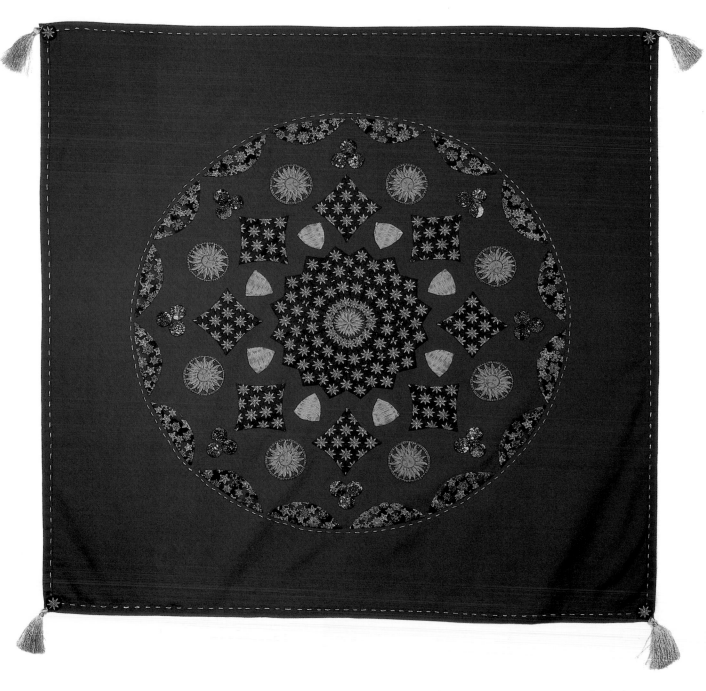

The Tasselled Tablecloth (page 74) uses the Kaleidoscope technique explained on pages 21–23.

If you need the answers to any other specific questions, you may find them in Basic Techniques (pages 17–32) or in the various Tip boxes scattered throughout the book.

Quilting, for many people, is an obsession which non-quilters find hard to understand. They say: 'You must need a great deal of patience.' But if you would rather quilt than do anything else in the world (almost), you don't need patience, because you are enjoying every moment of the creation of something beautiful.

BASIC TECHNIQUES

Here are some methods for that are used by quilters generally, for all types of work, and also some more specific techniques that I have developed for rose-window designs.

Basic Rose-Window Technique

For most rose-window quilts, you will need to find the centre of the backing fabric, and mark a circle, or circles, of the required size on the fabric.

1 The easiest way to do find the centre is to fold the fabric in half, first horizontally and then vertically. Mark the lines by pressing the fabric.

2 Then mark a circle of the desired size on the fabric. Use an appropriate marker, which will obviously depend on the colour of the background:
● when using a dark background, use a soapstone or chalk pencil
● if the background is a light colour, I usually use a water-erasable pen or a quilter's marking pencil.

3 Divide the circle into the necessary number of segments (see below) – measuring from the centre with a protractor – according to which window you are making.

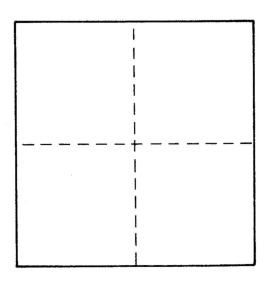

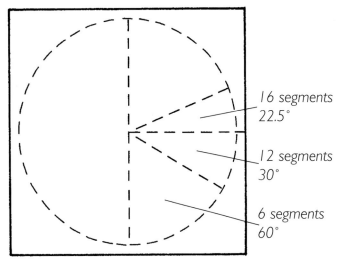

16 segments
22.5°

12 segments
30°

6 segments
60°

4 Draw lines, using the marker, from the centre to the edge of the circle. It is helpful to draw smaller concentric circles within the main one to help with placement of the pieces to be applied.

It is then advisable to go over the lines in tacking stitches, as the chalk will rub off and you will have to renew it, unless you are a very fast worker.

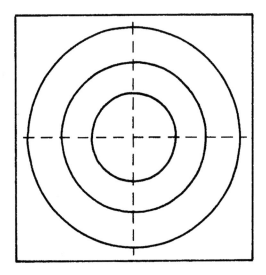

5 Trace the templates you want to use onto plastic, and cut them out carefully (see next page).

6 Decide which fabrics you want to use for each piece and cut them out, allowing about ¼ in (6 mm) all round for turnings (see next page).

7 Starting in the centre, arrange the pieces on the background. Pin them in place to make sure you are satisfied with the arrangement. (If you are designing your own window rather than basing your design on a real one, it's a good idea to cut your pieces in plain paper and arrange them on the background to make sure you are happy with the design, before cutting any fabric.)

8 Turn in the allowance on each piece, tack all around with small stitches and press the pieces carefully.

9 Re-pin the pieces on the background fabric, and sew them down with little invisible stitches, as shown below.

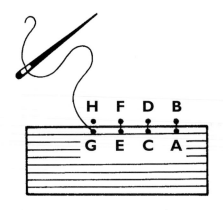

Bring needle from back at A. Replace needle at B, using the same hole as A, but only in background. Bring needle up at C, down at D, etc.

Making and Using Templates

No matter what sort of shapes you are making, you must always use a template of some sort.

If you want to make circles or ovals it is best, though not essential, to use a commercial template, sold by stationers', art or office supply shops. Using one of these means that you don't have to use a pair of compasses or measure anything. Just choose the size you need and draw inside the template.

For most other shapes (and for circles and for ovals if you wish) you must always make a template from template plastic. For the projects in this book, trace the shapes directly from the book onto the plastic.

Use either sort of template to cut out both interlining and fabric pieces.

FOR INTERLINING: mark the shape directly on the fabric and cut out. FOR FABRIC PIECES: mark the shape directly on the fabric, *add ¹/₄ in (6 mm) all round for turnings*, then cut out.

Making Circles, Ovals and Other Shapes

This time-saving technique can be used for many simple shapes: see right. However, there are some shapes which cannot be made like this: those with concave curves and those with sharp inward points: see below.

YES

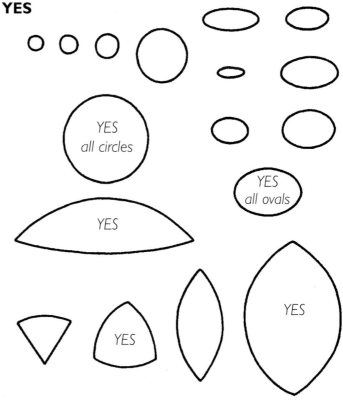

YES
all circles

YES
all ovals

YES

YES

YES

YES

YES: all squares, rectangles and triangles

NO

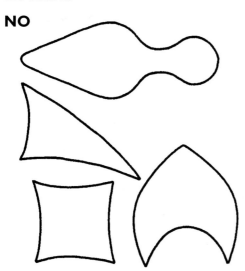

METHOD A: SHAPES WITH INTERLINING

Shapes made this way contain interlining which is left inside the fabric when finished.

1 Using the templates, draw the required number of shapes on interlining and cut out.

2 Using the same templates, draw the same shapes on the wrong side of your fabrics and cut out, allowing a little more than ¼ in (6 mm) all round for turning.

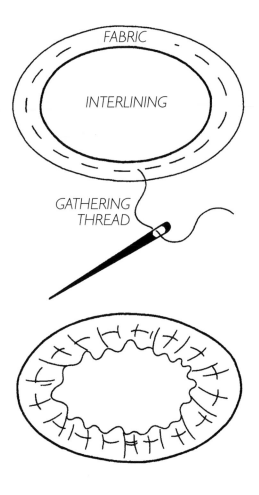

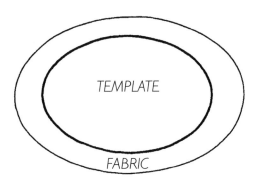

3 Stitch a gathering thread all round, close to the edge of the fabric (top right) and, with the interlining shape on the wrong side of the fabric, draw up the thread tightly and fasten off securely (above right). Press on both sides. When you have completed all the shapes, they are ready to be stitched onto the background.

METHOD B: SHAPES WITHOUT INTERLINING

If you don't want interlining inside the piece you are making – for instance, in a cushion cover or a bed quilt, which will at some time need to be washed – you should use thin card to make the shapes. Draw up the fabric as before, but this time around the card shape, and press firmly on both sides. Then cut the gathering thread, very carefully remove the card, tack around close to the folded edge of the piece you have made and again press firmly to retain the perfect shape. This is now ready to be sewn to the background.

Kaleidoscopes

Instead of the basic technique for making a rose-window quilt, I also have an alternative, favourite method which I call kaleidoscopes.

This involves making a piece very similar to a Dresden Plate, but using a fabric with a strong repeat, or a border fabric, and cutting each segment from the same part of the fabric pattern.

1 You must make a plastic template. Having decided how many segments you want in your design, calculate the shape of each piece by dividing 360° (the number of degrees in a circle) by the number of segments. For instance, if you want 16 segments in a circular pattern, the required angle is 22.5° (360 ÷ 16). Draw, on paper, the figure below (remember your geometry from school?).

For a kaleidoscope with 16 segments, draw a horizontal line, then measure up 22.5° from it with a protractor. Draw another line to make the angle. This will form the basis of each segment of the kaleidoscope.

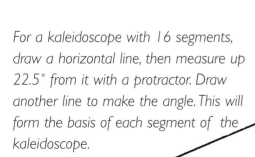

22.5°

2 Next, having decided on the diameter of the 'plate', measure half that distance from point A to points B and C. Then from B to C draw either a curve or two lines which meet at point D.

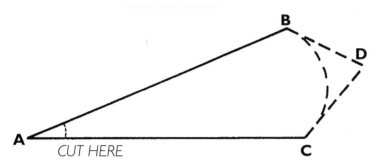

CUT HERE

NB: It will be easier to use the templates provided in the instructions for each project, but you should know how to do this in case you want more or fewer segments in your kaleidoscope.

Trace the template you have drawn onto plastic and cut ½ in (12 mm) from the tip.

3 Look at your chosen fabric and decide which part of the design you want to use. Place your template on the *wrong* side of the fabric. Trace a part of the fabric design onto the template with a permanent marker (as shown left). This is so you can place the template on exactly the same area of fabric pattern for the next piece.

4 Draw around the template. I tend to use the same marker unless I am using a light-coloured fabric, in which case I use a pencil. Move the template to the next place where the same part of the fabric pattern appears (see right) and, placing your template exactly in the same position, and making sure you have left enough space for about ¼ in (6 mm) turnings, draw around the template again. Repeat until you have enough pieces for the kaleidoscope. This may seem to be very wasteful, but you can usually cut pieces for another kaleidoscope from the remaining fabric by using your template the other way up (see page 23).

5 Now we have arrived at the exciting part: joining the pieces together. This is exciting because you're never quite sure what will happen until you've stitched a couple of seams. First, place two pieces right sides together, putting pins in at right angles to the marked line (see below). Push each pin in on the marked line, ensuring that it comes out on the same part of the design on the other side.

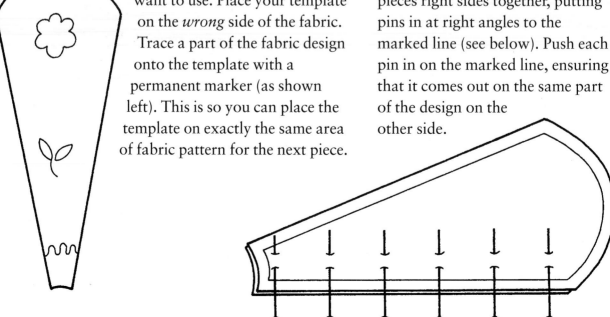

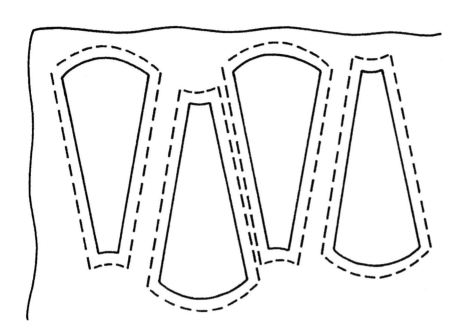

6 When you are sure that it is correctly pinned, stitch, either by hand or machine, from A to B, leaving about ¼ in (6 mm) unstitched at A (see below). Remove the pins and open out. Continue to join the pieces until you have completed the circle.

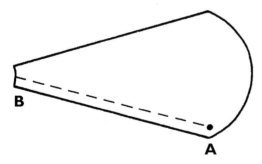

7 Iron on the wrong side, pressing all the seams in the same direction. If the circle doesn't lie flat in the centre, take the seams in a little – by just a couple of fabric threads – starting half way down. If, on the other hand, the circle doesn't lie

flat at the outer edge, take the seams in at the outer part of the circle (see below). Press again.

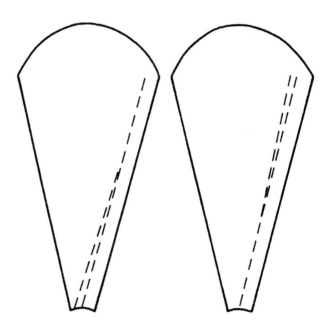

8 Turn in the allowance around the outer edge and press. You are now ready to stitch your kaleidoscope onto the background.

Quilting

A quilt traditionally consists of three layers: top, wadding and backing. Of course, both quilting and appliqué can be done by machine, but I prefer to work by hand. (Also, I'm not very good at either by machine.)

1   Cut the backing and wadding 2–3 in (5–7.5 cm) larger all round than the finished top. Lay the backing, wrong side up, on your work surface, then the wadding and finally the quilt top, right side up.

2   Starting in the middle, put rows of pins from side to side of the quilt, about 4 in (10 cm) apart.

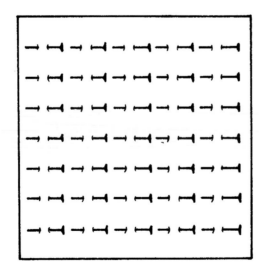

3   Again, beginning in the middle, work rows of tacking across the quilt, remove the pins, turn the work round and work another row of tacking in the other direction, so that you have a grid of tacking (see below).

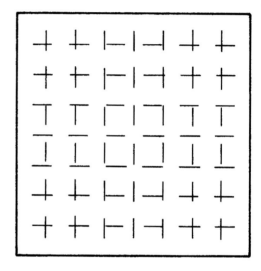

4   Start quilting in the centre of the work. The quilting stitch is a small running stitch, which must go through all three layers, and the stitches should be the same size on the back as on the front.

5   To begin, make a small knot in the end of the thread and slide the needle between the layers, bring it up where you want to begin quilting. Give the thread a gentle tug and the knot will disappear into the wadding.

6 When you come to the end of the quilting, or to the end of the thread, wind the thread around the needle two or three times, as though you were making a French knot, and work the knot close to the fabric. Slip the needle between the layers for about 1 in (2.5 cm), pull the knot into the wadding and cut the thread. This technique, usually known as 'popping the knot', avoids any knots showing on the back or the front of the work.

Types of quilting

Outline quilting (below) is done ¼ in (6 mm) inside the patches.

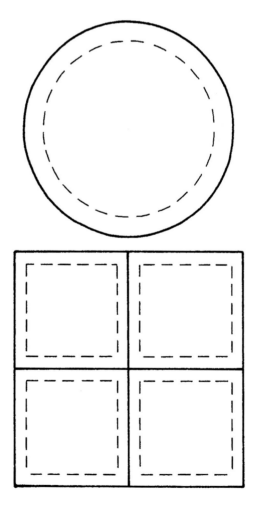

Quilting **'in the ditch'** is sewn very close to the seam, on the side which does not have the seam allowance: seams are usually pressed to one side when quilts are pieced (sewn together).

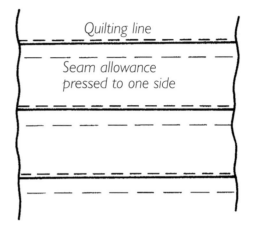

Quilting line

Seam allowance pressed to one side

Vermicelli quilting (below) is that which wanders about, the curved lines never crossing, and looks very effective. It is possible to buy a stencil for this, but it isn't too difficult to draw onto your work. Just in case you don't know, vermicelli means 'little worms', but don't let me put you off your pasta!

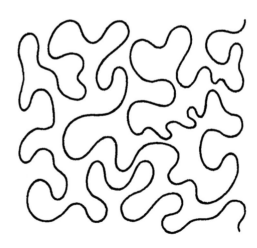

Trapunto: Stuffed or Corded Quilting

The instructions here concentrate on corded work. Two rows of quilting, about ¼ in (6 mm) apart, are worked, and then a cord is threaded between them. I use double (8-ply) knitting yarn, double, for the cord. You will also need a trapunto needle, which is usually about 6 in (15 cm) long and has a large eye. (A large-eyed tapestry needle may be used instead.) It is best if the backing fabric is fairly loosely woven.

1 Draw the chosen design on the top fabric before you make the quilt 'sandwich', then quilt once around the motif.

2 Work a second row of quilting ¼ in (6 mm) inside the first row of stitches.

3 Thread the trapunto needle with a double length of thick knitting yarn and, from the back of the work, push the needle between the two rows of quilting.

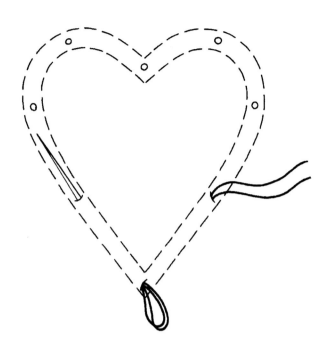

4 Continue to push, feeding the yarn through the channel, rather like threading knicker elastic (if anyone does that these days), until you reach a corner or a tight curve. Push the needle to the back and pull the yarn through the channel until the end of it reaches the entry hole. Don't let it go right into the channel, or you will have to pull it out and begin again.

5 Put the needle back into the same hole and proceed as before, leaving a short tail of the yarn outside the hole (see above right).

6 Continue in this way until you have completed the motif, cut the yarn close to the final exit and stretch the work to eliminate puckers. Press on the wrong side over a towel.

Corners and Borders

All the wall-hangings in this book are square or rectangular so attention needs to be given to the corners. The 'Washington' Wall-Hanging (page 102) has vermicelli quilting in the corners, which was tedious to do, but worth the effort. (See Types of Quilting, page 25.)

One of my rose windows (not in this book) has a rose quilted in each corner, and many corner stencils are available if you don't want to design your own.

Suggested designs for corners are butterflies; hearts; flowers; toys or animals for a child's quilt; or abstracts. Some examples are shown on the right.

Another way to decorate the corners is to repeat some of the shapes and fabrics used in the main part of the Window. A few examples are shown right, on page 29, as well as various other ideas for filling corners.

Two of the quilts in this book are rectangular and I have used a different method for each of them. The 'Chartres' Wall-Hanging (page 108) has Gothic window shapes in varying heights used at the top and bottom of the rose, and 'Come to the Fair' Wall-Hanging (page 56) has a border top and bottom. Templates for these are given in the instructions for the quilts, but there are several other ideas on these pages.

Hanging a quilt

SLEEVE AND ROD

The most common and probably the simplest way of hanging a quilt is to attach a 'sleeve' to the back of the quilt, through which a rod can be pushed. It is not enough just to sew a length of fabric to the back as

● the rod could eventually wear the fibres of the quilt, and

● the rod makes the front of the quilt bulge outwards.

1 Cut a piece from backing fabric that measures 5 in (12.5 cm) by the width of your hanging.

2 Fold it in half lengthways and press. Open it out and fold the long edges to the centre. Press the folds firmly. (Do not lose these folds: they will be the stitching lines.) Make narrow hems on the short edges.

3 Now place the long edges right sides together and sew a ½ in (12 mm) seam, making a tube. *Finger* press the seam open and turn to the right side.

4 Place the tube, with the seam to the back, just below the binding of

your quilt (on the back, of course); pin, and hand stitch along the fold you made earler. Then pin and stitch the other fold to the quilt. You will see that you now have created a space for the rod to go in without distorting the quilt's front.

5 Use a length of ¾ in (2 cm) diameter dowel, a little shorter than the width of the quilt. Screw two metal eyes to the ends. (Remember that you made hems on the ends of the sleeve: this means that the sleeve is a little shorter than the quilt.)

6 Put two nails in the wall at the same distance apart as the screw eyes, thread the dowel through the sleeve and hang your quilt. The dowel shouldn't show at all and the quilt will appear to float on the wall with no visible means of support.

LOOPS WITH DECORATIVE POLE

You can also hang your quilt with loops, as I have done for the 'Come to the Fair' Wall-Hanging (page 56).

If doing this method, it's a nice touch to put little wooden finials on the ends of the dowel, and hang it on ornamental hooks.

1 Cut a strip of fabric 42 x 3½ in (108 x 9 cm) from the background fabric.

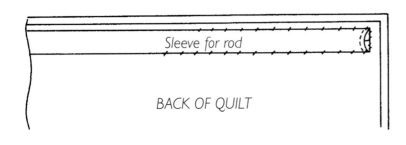

Sleeve for rod

BACK OF QUILT

2 Place the long edges right sides together and sew a ¼ in (6 mm) seam along the long edge. Turn and press, with the seam positioned in the centre.

3 Cut the strip into six pieces, each 7 in (18 cm) long. Fold these pieces in half, turning the raw edges to the inside, and sew to the top of the quilt, spacing them equally.

Binding a Quilt

The simplest way of binding a square or rectangular quilt is to cut the backing fabric 3–4 in (7.5–10 cm) larger than the background fabric all the way round. When the quilting is complete, fold the backing over the font, turn the edges in and stich down. However, I find that this method is not always satisfactory, as the quilting pulls the work in and the bound edge becomes wavy. I prefer to use the following system:

STRIP BINDING
1 Measure the quilted piece across the centre in both directions.

2 Cut two pieces of fabric, either in the backing fabric or in a contrasting colour, the length of the vertical sides by 2½ in (6.5 cm) wide. Fold and press in half lengthways.

3 Use double to bind the sides: place the binding's raw edges to the edge of the quilt, pin, and stitch with a ¼ in (6 mm) seam. Turn the binding over the seam allowance and hand stitch on the back.

4 Cut another two pieces of fabric about 1 in (2.5 cm) longer than the horizontal measurement and bind the top and bottom in the same way, turning in the excess fabric at the ends.

FACING
Recently, I have been facing my quilts instead of binding them, which gives a pleasant finish.

Cut the facings in the same way as the bindings, wider if you wish, but turn the whole facing right to the back of the quilt before stitching it down.

In 'Sarah's Quilt' (see page 94) I have used a contrasting facing.

BINDING CURVED EDGES
Of course, if you have curved edges on your quilt, you must use a bias binding so that the fabric is able to stretch around the curved sides of the quilt.

Either make your own – cutting strips of cloth on the diagonal bias – which means that it can be whatever colour and width you wish. Alternatively, use purchased binding which is available in a wide range of colours and various widths as well.

Making Cushion Covers

The overlapping method of closing a cushion cover is the simplest – although you can use a zip, Velcro or buttons if you wish.

1 For a square cushion, cut two rectangles in backing fabric: the width of the cushion plus 1 in (2.5 cm), by the width plus 4–5 in (10–12.5 cm), and make narrow hems on one long side of each piece.

2 Place the finished cushion top, right side up, on a work surface, then arrange the two rectangles wrong side up, so that the edges are level, and the backing pieces overlap in the middle (see below).

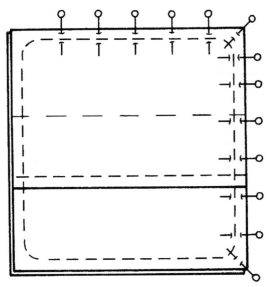

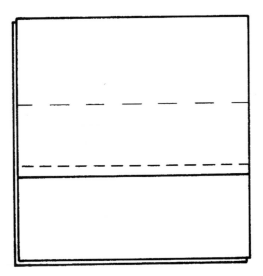

3 Pin around all four edges, then stitch all round the outside, rounding off the corners slightly (top right).

4 Trim the seam and neaten by zig-zagging all round. Turn to the right side and press.

ROUND CUSHION COVERS
Make a round cushion in the same way, but overlap the two rectangles, and pin them in the centre, before cutting the backing into a circle to match the cushion top. Then finish the sewing as for a square cushion (below).

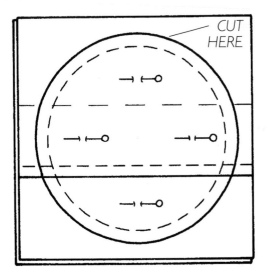

CUT HERE

The projects shown here range from very simple designs to those based on real windows, which are more complex. Follow the instructions carefully and you will be able to complete beautiful accessories for your home, and for special gifts for friends and relations.

Window of Rainbows

Either small prints or plain fabrics may be used for this framed picture. Colours of the rainbow could provide a bright spot for a dull corner in a living room, or they could suggest a possible colour scheme for a child's room.

MATERIALS

22 in (56 cm) square cream-coloured cotton fabric for background

12 x 3 in (30 x 7.5 cm) approx of cotton fabrics in red, orange, yellow, green, blue and purple

3½ yd (3.2 m) ¼ in (6 mm) adhesive bias tape in gold

⅛ yd (11.5 cm) pelmet interfacing or other heavy interfacing such as Craft Vilene

22 in (56 cm) square 2 oz (50 g) wadding

22 in (56 cm) square cream or white cotton for backing

Cream sewing thread

EQUIPMENT

Basic sewing kit (needles, pins, scissors, tacking thread, etc)

Pencil for marking design on fabric

Ruler

Pair of compasses

Protractor

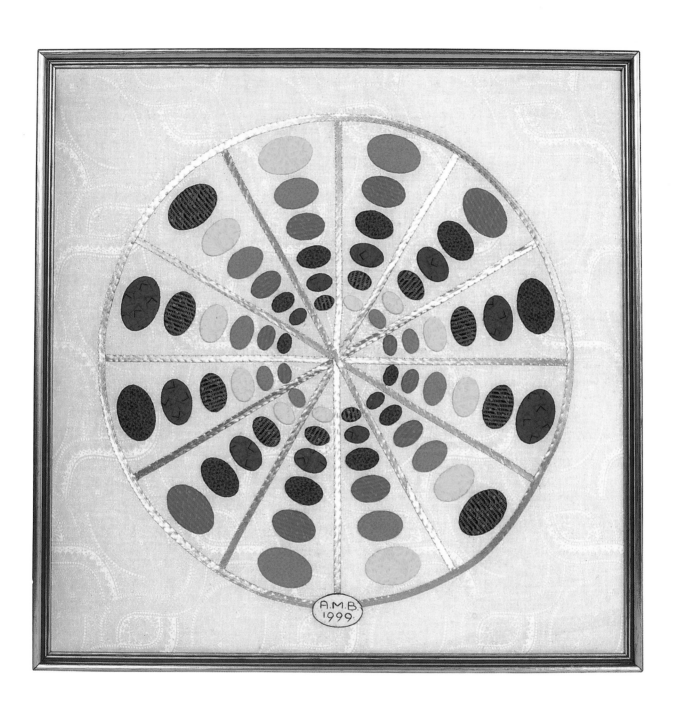

PREPARING THE DESIGN

1 Fold and press the fabric to find the centre as shown Basic Technique (page 17).

2 On the *back* of the fabric, (so the marks won't show on the front) mark a circle with a radius of 8½ in (21.5 cm). Using the protractor, divide it into 12 segments (30° each), to show where the patches should be placed.

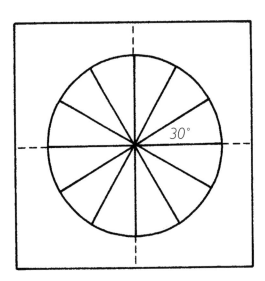

3 Tack along all the lines so that they show on the front (below).

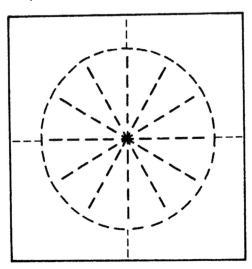

MAKING THE WINDOW

4 Cut two ovals in each size, in each of the six colours, allowing ¼ in (6 mm) for turnings all round. Cut 12 ovals in each size in interfacing.

TEMPLATES: Actual size

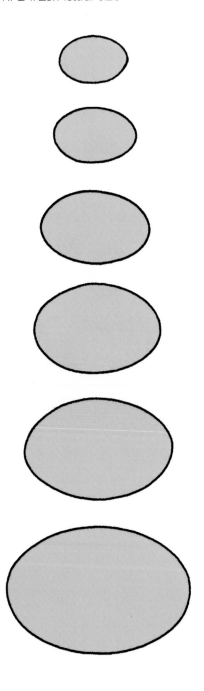

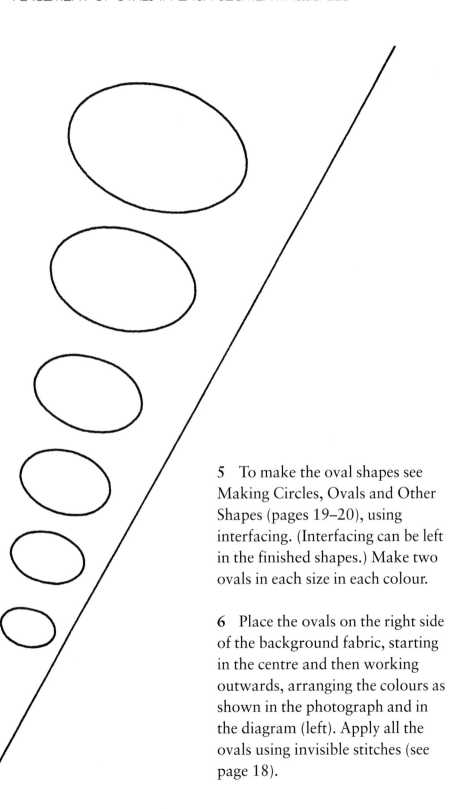

PLACEMENT OF OVALS IN EACH SEGMENT: *Actual size*

8½ in (21.5 cm)

5   To make the oval shapes see Making Circles, Ovals and Other Shapes (pages 19–20), using interfacing. (Interfacing can be left in the finished shapes.) Make two ovals in each size in each colour.

6   Place the ovals on the right side of the background fabric, starting in the centre and then working outwards, arranging the colours as shown in the photograph and in the diagram (left). Apply all the ovals using invisible stitches (see page 18).

7 Cut six 16½ in (42 cm) lengths of gold bias tape, iron in place over each row of straight tacking and stitch down.

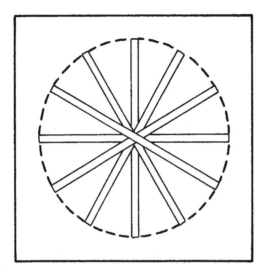

8 Pin bias tape around the circle, starting at point A and working your way carefully around until you are back at the beginning. Trim the other pieces of bias where necessary. Starting on the inside edge of the bias tape, stitch the tape around the circle. Then stitch on the outside edge.

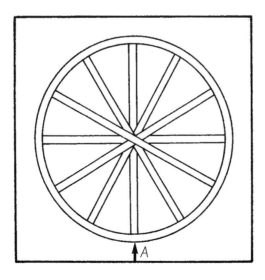

TIP

Ironing bias tape

Gold bias tape melts if the iron is too hot. Test a small piece of it on a spare scrap of fabric.

9 Cut an oval from a small piece of background fabric or calico, write your initials and the date on it, either with a fabric pen or with embroidery. Gather it onto an oval cut from interfacing (see page 20) and stitch it over the join in the bias tape at point A.

10 Press the finished picture on the wrong side. Make the quilting 'sandwich' (see Quilting, page 24), pin and stitch it all the way round. Press it on the wrong side again, and your picture is ready to be framed.

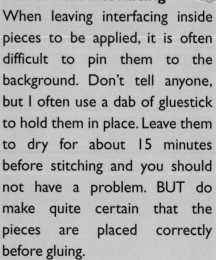

TIP

Pieces with interfacing

When leaving interfacing inside pieces to be applied, it is often difficult to pin them to the background. Don't tell anyone, but I often use a dab of gluestick to hold them in place. Leave them to dry for about 15 minutes before stitching and you should not have a problem. BUT do make quite certain that the pieces are placed correctly before gluing.

Small Cushion

Several of these little cushions could add a sparkle to a plain-coloured sofa or divan.

MATERIALS

Two 15 in (38 cm) squares black cotton fabric for the background and backing

15 in (38 cm) square thin cotton fabric for lining

½ yd (45 cm) cotton fabric with a repeat pattern or border print

Small scraps of two contrasting fabrics

2 yd (2 m) ½ in (6 mm) black iron-on bias tape

15 in (38 cm) square thin wadding

14 in (35 cm) square cushion pad

Black thread for quilting

EQUIPMENT

Basic sewing kit (needles, pins, scissors, tacking thread, etc)

Template plastic

Ruler

Pair of compasses

PREPARING THE DESIGN

1   Fold and press the fabric to find the centre as shown below and in Basic Techniques (see page 17). Also fold and mark the diagonals.

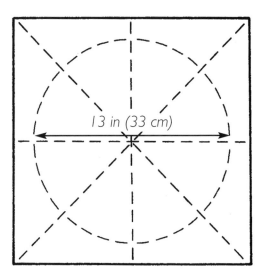

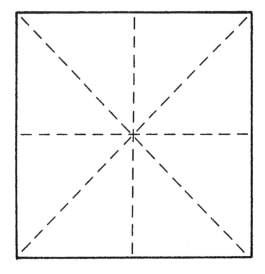

2   Mark a 13 in (33 cm) circle on the background square.

3   Make plastic templates, tracing them from the template diagram. Using only template 1, cut the shape from the patterned fabrics, adding ¼ in (6 mm) all round for turnings.

TEMPLATES: Actual size

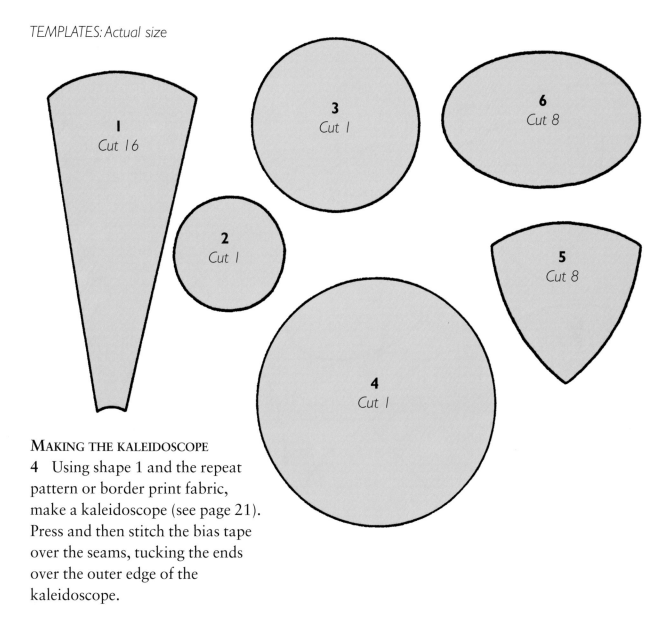

MAKING THE KALEIDOSCOPE

4 Using shape 1 and the repeat pattern or border print fabric, make a kaleidoscope (see page 21). Press and then stitch the bias tape over the seams, tucking the ends over the outer edge of the kaleidoscope.

5 Cut one circle in a contrasting colour using template 2, one black circle from template 3 and another contrasting one from template 4. (Remember to add ¼ in (6 mm) all round for turnings. Make up the circles (see Making Circles, Ovals and Other Shapes, page 20). Place them one on top of the other (right) and stitch them together. Press and stitch them over the centre of the kaleidoscope.

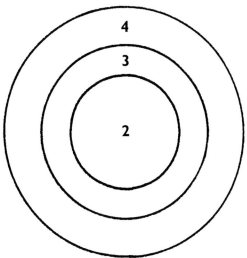

QUARTER OF DESIGN: Actual size

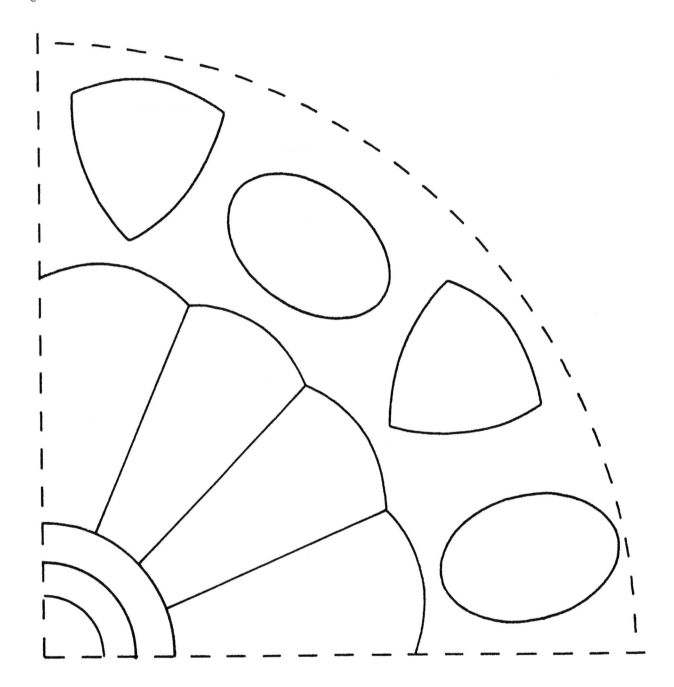

APPLIQUE AND QUILTING

6   Using the pressed folds as a guide, place the finished kaleidoscope on the background. Pin and stitch in position.

7   Cut patches from templates 5 and 6, adding ¼ in (6 mm) all round for turnings, using other parts of the border print. Make them up (see page 20). Arrange the patches on the background as shown above and stitch in place.

8   Make the quilting 'sandwich' (see Quilting, page 24). Quilt around the kaleidoscope and the patches. Finally, quilt around the outer circle.

MAKING UP

9   Make up the cushion cover (see Making Cushion Covers, page 32). Insert the cushion pad.

TIP
Choosing needles

Most quilters use the traditional quilters' needles (known as 'Betweens'). These needles are very short indeed and I have finally given up using them. I use 'Sharps' which are slightly longer and I find I have much more control. Try them, both for quilting and for appliqué.

Market-Day Bag

*While hunting through my boxes for fabrics to use on this bag,
I found that I had quite a collection of fruit and
vegetable prints, which seemed to be perfect.
However, any 'theme' fabrics would be just as good:
animals, flowers, stars, etc.
A 'tidy' bag for a child's room could be appliquéd with toys.*

MATERIALS

Two 19 x 19 in (48 x 48 cm) squares background fabric

Two 20 in (51 cm) squares thin wadding

Two 20 in (51 cm) squares thin cotton for back of quilting

Two 20 in (51 cm) squares printed cotton for bag lining

Selection of 'fat quarters' or scraps for appliqué (see Tip, page 50)

Heavy interlining for making appliqué shapes

4 yd (4 m) approx thick knitting yarn

Quilting thread

EQUIPMENT

Basic sewing kit (needles, pins, scissors, tacking thread, etc)

Sewing machine (optional)

Trapunto needle

Ruler

Pair of compasses

Chalk/soapstone pencil

MAKING THE SIDES

1   Fold and press the fabric to find the centre as shown in Basic Technique (see page 17). Also fold and mark the diagonals. Mark circles with radii of 7, 4½ and 3 in (18, 11.5 and 7.5 cm).

2   Make a plastic template for each of the shapes in the template diagram. Using these templates, cut the required number of shapes from the interlining.

3   Select the fabrics for each side of the bag and cut out the shapes, remembering to allow ¼ in (6 mm) all round for turning. Make up all the shapes and press carefully (see Making Circles, Ovals and Other Shapes, pages 19–20).

4   Arrange the correct shapes on one side of the bag (see pages 48–49). Pin, and stitch in place (see Step 8, page 18). Repeat for the other side of the bag.

5   When both sides are complete, make the quilting sandwich (see Quilting, page 24) and quilt just outside each shape. Finally quilt two rows around the outer circle and cord (see Trapunto, page 26).

FRUIT TEMPLATES: Actual size

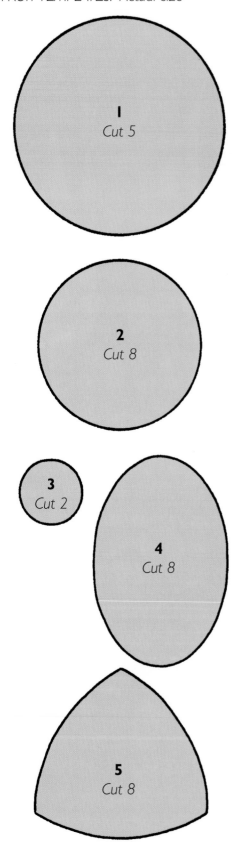

1
Cut 5

2
Cut 8

3
Cut 2

4
Cut 8

5
Cut 8

VEGETABLE TEMPLATES: Actual size

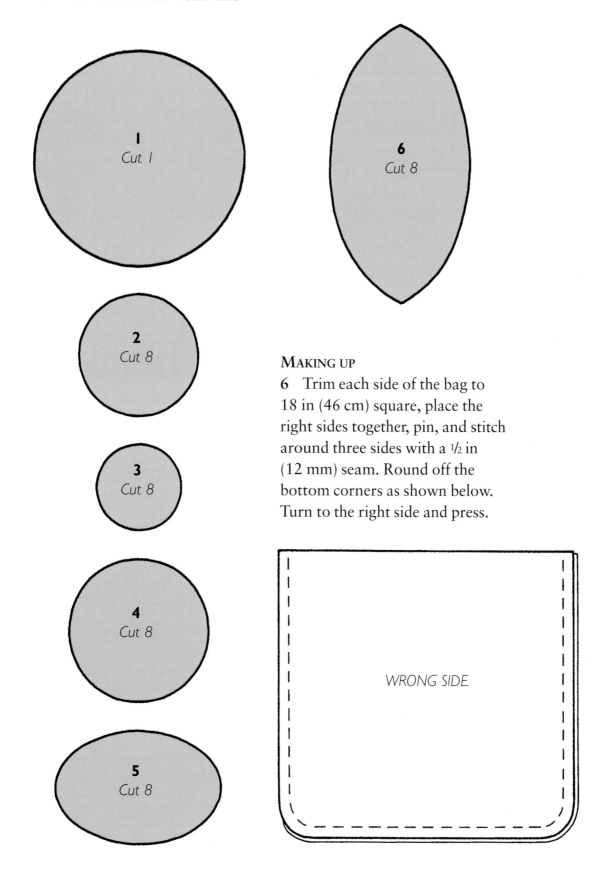

1
Cut 1

6
Cut 8

2
Cut 8

3
Cut 8

4
Cut 8

5
Cut 8

MAKING UP

6   Trim each side of the bag to 18 in (46 cm) square, place the right sides together, pin, and stitch around three sides with a ½ in (12 mm) seam. Round off the bottom corners as shown below. Turn to the right side and press.

WRONG SIDE

FRUIT SIDE: QUARTER OF DESIGN: Actual size

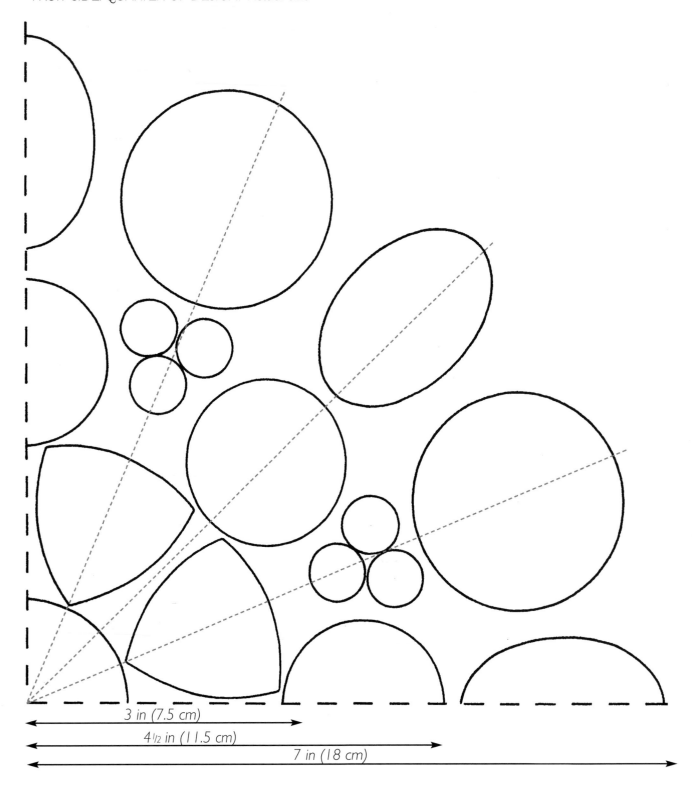

3 in (7.5 cm)

4½ in (11.5 cm)

7 in (18 cm)

VEGETABLE SIDE: QUARTER OF DESIGN: Actual size

3 in (7.5 cm)

4 ½ in (11.5 cm)

7 in (18 cm)

7   To make the handles, from the remaining background fabric cut two pieces 10 x 24 in (25 x 61 cm). Fold in half lengthways and press. Fold the long edges to the middle, press and then fold in half and press again. Pin, and sew four rows of machine stitching from end to end on each piece as shown below.

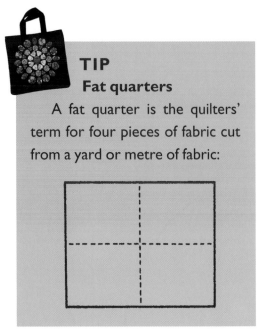

TIP
Fat quarters
A fat quarter is the quilters' term for four pieces of fabric cut from a yard or metre of fabric:

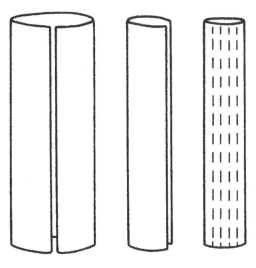

8   Place one handle on each side of the bag, pin, and sew in place with two or three rows of machine stitching.

9   From the lining fabric cut two 18½ in (47 cm) squares. Place right sides together and stitch as shown on page 49. Turn the upper edges of the bag over by ½ in (12 mm), pin, and work two or three rows of machine stitching all round the top, sewing carefully across the handles, so as not to break the machine needle. Result: a useful and unique bag.

RIGHT SIDE

Simple Cushion
or
Wall-Hanging

This colourful cushion makes a bright focal point in any room or, made in Christmas fabrics, it would be a delightful Christmas gift.

MATERIALS

22 in (56 cm) square black cotton fabric

Several fat quarters (see Tip, page 50) or scraps of brightly coloured cotton fabric

22 in (56 cm) square 2 oz (50 g) wadding

22 in (56 cm) square thin cotton fabric for lining

22 x 32 in (56 x 81 cm) black cotton fabric for back of cushion

Black sewing thread

Black quilting thread

20 in (50 cm) cushion pad

EQUIPMENT

Basic sewing kit (needles, pins, scissors, tacking thread, etc.)

Sewing machine

Template plastic

Ruler

Pair of compasses

Chalk/soapstone pencil

PREPARING THE DESIGN

1   Fold and press the fabric to find the centre as shown in Basic Technique (see page 17). Also fold and mark the diagonals.

2   Use your compasses to draw an 8½ in (21.5 cm) radius circle, and then a 5¾ in (14.5cm) radius circle (below). These will help you to place the patches accurately.

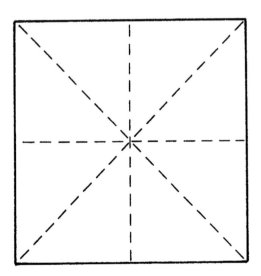
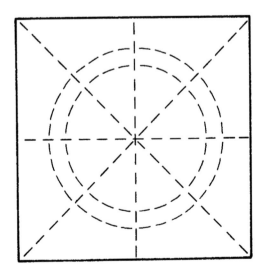

APPLIQUE AND QUILTING

3 Trace the templates 1–5 (right) on to the template plastic and cut them out carefully.

4 Decide which fabric you want to use for each patch and use the templates to cut the correct number of patches from the appropriate fabrics. Remember to add ¼ in (6 mm) all round for turnings. You will need to cut one large circle for the centre and eight of each of the other shapes.

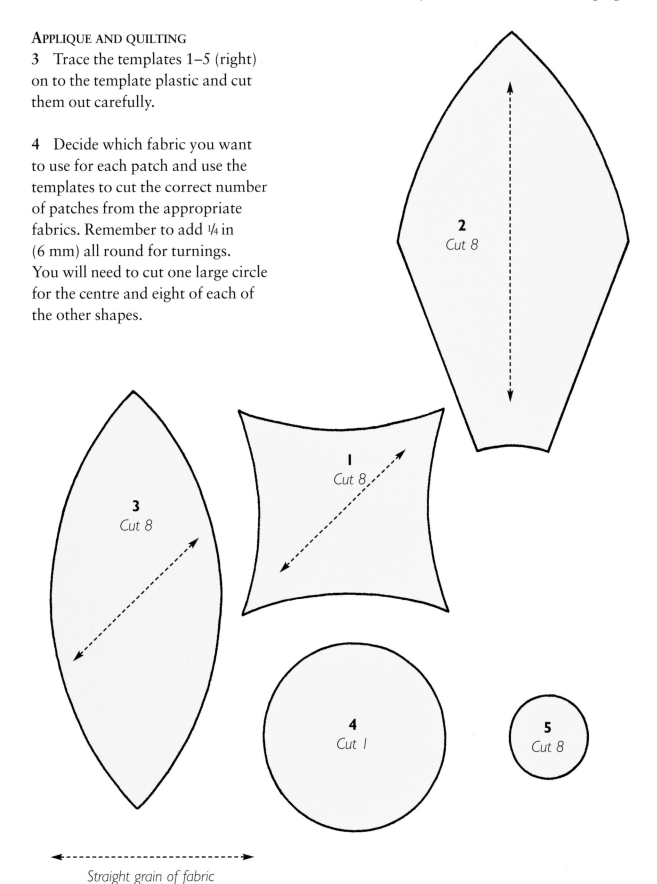

Straight grain of fabric

5 Turn in the seam allowance on each patch (see Making Circles, Ovals and Other Shapes, page 20).

6 Place the patches on the backing so that you can see the finished effect; use the marked lines and circles to help you to place them correctly. Fold shapes 2 and 3 in half, unfold them and place them with the folds along the chalk lines.

7 When you are satisfied with the arrangement, pin or tack the pieces in position and stitch them in place, starting in the centre and working outwards. Use a blind stitch (see page 18). When you have sewn all the patches on, gently rub the fabric with a clean cloth to remove any remaining chalk marks. Press the entire piece of work.

8 Make the quilting 'sandwich' (see Quilting, page 24). Pin and tack as shown, and then quilt with small running stitches, about 1/8 in (3 mm) outside each patch, beginning as always in the centre of the piece of work and working outwards. Finally, quilt around the outer circle of the whole design.

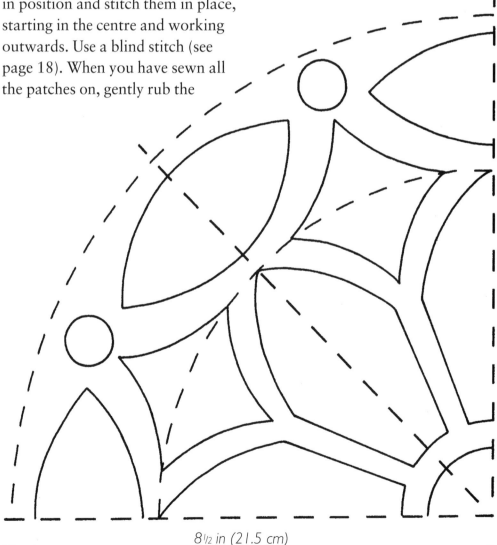

8 1/2 in (21.5 cm)

TIP
Avoiding sore fingers

If your 'underneath' finger becomes sore when you are quilting, wrap a piece of narrow masking tape a couple of times around the tip. You will still be able to feel the point of the needle but it won't prick your finger and make it painful.

MAKING UP

To make a square wall-hanging, bind the raw edges, and sew a sleeve on the back (see Hanging a Quilt and Binding, pages 30–31).

For instructions on making up a cushion cover see page 32. To make a round cushion, trim the quilted piece to a 19 in (48 cm) circle before stitching the seams and finishing.

'Come to the Fair' Wall-Hanging

*I thought I had completed all the projects for this book
when I saw these lovely fabrics at a quilt show.
They cried out to be made into a rose-window quilt
so, of course, I bought some.
The finished hanging reminded my husband
and some of my friends of a fairground – hence the title.*

MATERIALS

1 yd (1 m) 45 in (115 cm) cotton for background, binding and
    hanging loops
1 yd (1 m) 45 in (115 cm) cotton for backing
36 x 28in (91 x 71 cm) thin wadding
4 or 5 'fat quarters' printed fabrics (see Tip, page 50)
Heavy interfacing
Quilting thread

EQUIPMENT

Basic sewing kit (needles, pins, scissors, tacking thread, etc)
Template plastic
Ruler
Pair of compasses

PREPARING THE DESIGN

1   From the background fabric cut a rectangle 36 x 28 in (91 x 71cm). Fold and press the fabric to find the centre as shown in Basic Technique (see page 17). Mark a circle with a 12 in (30.5 cm) radius.

2   Using the protractor, divide the circle into 12 segments (30° each), (see Basic Technique, page 17). Then mark two more circles with radii of 6½ and 8½ in (16.5 and 21.5 cm), to help with placement of patches.

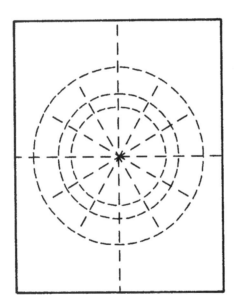

3   Make plastic templates, tracing them from the template diagram and remembering to add ¼ in (6 mm) for turnings. (If you have ready-made plastic templates for ovals and circles, use these to draw templates 1, 2A, 6, 8, and 9 straight on to interfacing. These may be left inside the finished piece). Cut out carefully.

APPLIQUE AND QUILTING

4   Decide which fabrics you want to use for each part of the design and cut out the patches, remembering to add ¼ in (6 mm) for turnings.

5   Make up shapes 1, 2A, 4, 6, 8 and 9 with interlining as shown in Making Circles, Ovals and Other Shapes, page 20. Turn in the edges of the other pieces and tack, but DO NOT turn in the curved edge on template 2B or the short edges on pieces 5 and 7. Place piece 2A to overlap the raw edge of piece 2B and stitch in place.

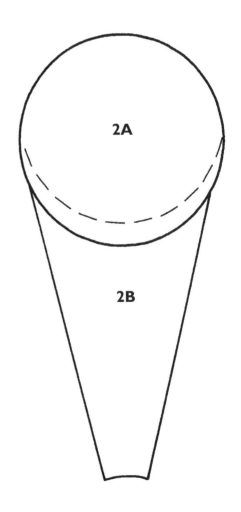

TEMPLATES: *Actual size*

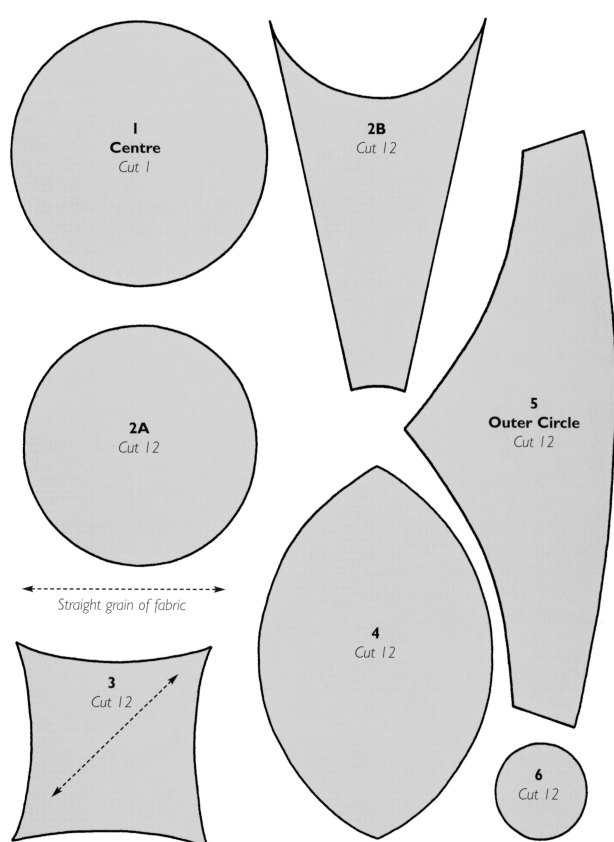

I
Centre
Cut 1

2B
Cut 12

2A
Cut 12

5
Outer Circle
Cut 12

Straight grain of fabric

3
Cut 12

4
Cut 12

6
Cut 12

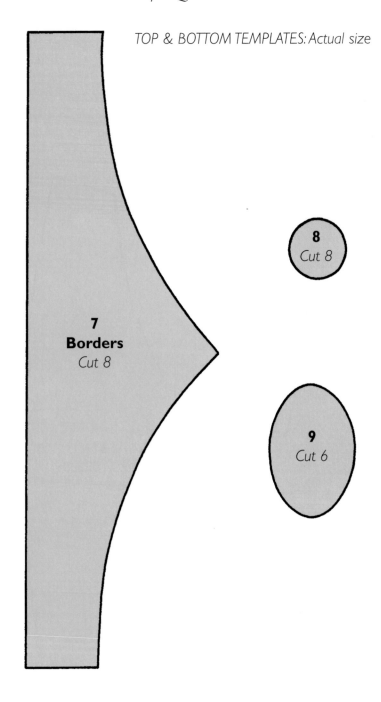

TOP & BOTTOM TEMPLATES: Actual size

7 Borders *Cut 8*

8 *Cut 8*

9 *Cut 6*

PART OF TOP BORDER

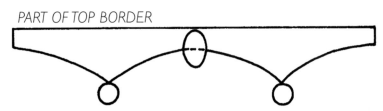

6 Starting in the centre, arrange pieces 1, 2A and 2B, 3, and 4 on the background and stitch in place. Arrange the shape 5 pieces around the outer circle so that they fit, overlapping or trimming where necessary. Stitch, and cover the joins with the small shape 6 circles.

7 Press the work and then draw horizontal lines top and bottom, 4 in (10 cm) above and below the circle (see right). Arrange the shape 7 pieces on these lines, four at the top and four at the bottom, over-lapping or trimming as before. Arrange the shape 9 ovals over the joins and sew the small circles (shape 8) at the points (below left).

8 Make the quilting 'sandwich' (see Quilting, page 24) and quilt around each patch and the borders.

MAKING UP

9 From the remaining back-ground fabric or prints cut out six pieces 4 x 7 in (10 x 18 cm) and make into hanging loops (see Hanging a Quilt, pages 30–31). Make the binding from back-ground, backing or print fabrics. Then sew on the loops and 'Come to the Fair'!

PLAN OF WALL-HANGING: *To scale*

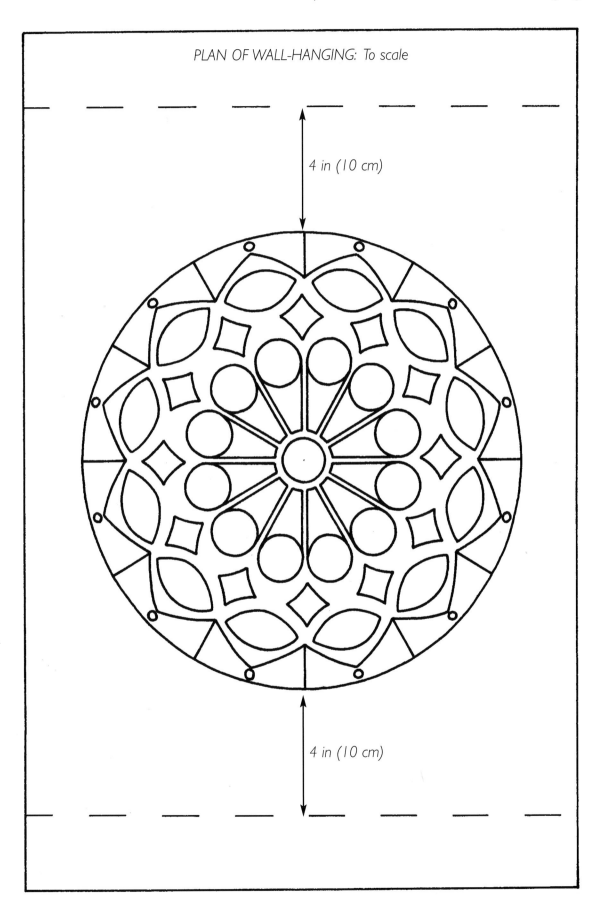

4 in (10 cm)

4 in (10 cm)

Trapunto Cushions

*This charming design is taken from a rose window in France,
and looks like an Art Nouveau design,
although I don't know the actual date of the window.
Because I didn't want to tackle so many sharp points in appliqué,
I have made it in trapunto and in shadow quilting (see page 68).
You will also find this design worked in appliqué in the
'Guest' Artistes section of the book as Art Nouveau Wall-Hanging.*

MATERIALS

20 in (51 cm) square fabric for front of cushion

20 in (51 cm) square thin fabric for first lining

20 in (51 cm) square thin wadding

20 in (51 cm) square thin fabric for final lining of cushion,
   to cover back of trapunto

20 x 25 in (51 x 64 cm) fabric for back of cushion

6 in (40 cm) iron-on Velcro

18 in (45 cm) diameter round cushion pad, OR
   18 in (45 cm) square cushion pad

Quilting thread, matching or contrasting with main fabric

Thick knitting yarn

EQUIPMENT

Basic sewing kit (needles, pins, scissors, tacking thread, etc)

Template plastic

Trapunto needle

Ruler

Pair of compasses

Round Cushion

PREPARING THE DESIGN

1   From the background fabric cut a rectangle 36 x 28 in (91 x 71cm). Fold and press the fabric to find the centre as shown in Basic Technique (see page 17). Using this point, mark a circle with an 8 in (20 cm) radius.

2   If you are using light-coloured fabric you can now trace the design directly on to it, using the pressed folds as a guide. With dark fabric it is best to make plastic templates (see Making and Using Templates, page 19, and page 66) and draw around them directly onto the fabric with a soapstone or chalk pencil ensuring that they are accurately positioned.

QUILTING AND TRAPUNTO

3   Make the quilting 'sandwich' (see Quilting, page 24). Using quilting thread, and starting in the centre, quilt around all the shapes, and then quilt another line ¼ in (6 mm) inside each shape as shown in Trapunto, page 26. Stitch a double row of quilting around the outer circle.

4   Use a double thickness of knitting yarn in the trapunto needle and fill all the double lines, easing the channels so that they are not puckered.

5   Cut around the finished design, about 1 in (2.5 cm) from the outer circle. From the final lining fabric cut a 16 in (40.5 cm) circle, put the quilted piece on top of it and tack all round, close to the edge.

Square Cushion

You will need the same amount of fabrics as for the round cushion, plus an 18 in (45 cm) square cushion pad. I used shot silk which appears to change colour according to the way light falls on it.

Work the trapunto as before (see Trapunto, page 26) and when the cording is complete cut the cushion top to an 18 in (45 cm) square.

MAKING UP
Make up the cushion cover, following the instructions in Making Cushion Covers, page 32.

TEMPLATES: *Actual size*

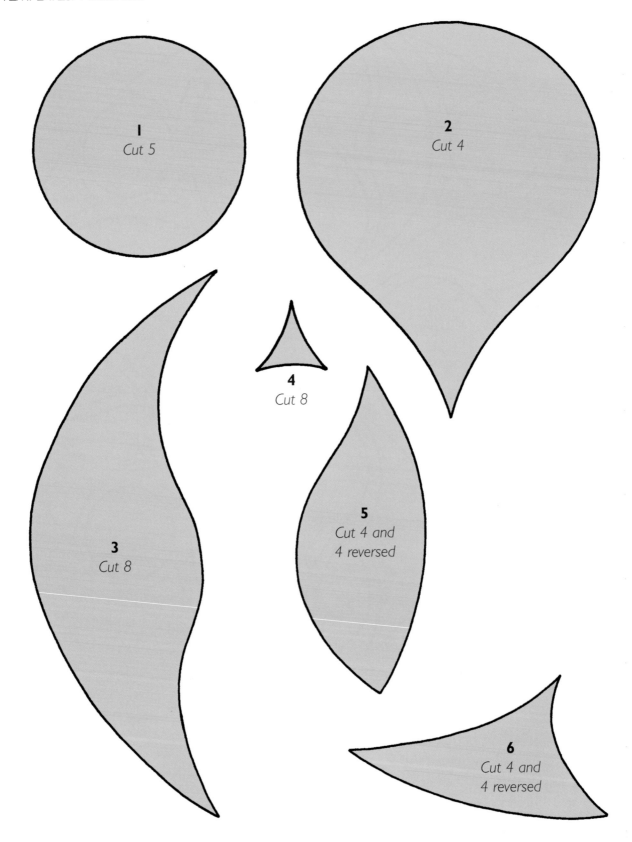

1
Cut 5

2
Cut 4

4
Cut 8

3
Cut 8

5
*Cut 4 and
4 reversed*

6
*Cut 4 and
4 reversed*

QUARTER OF DESIGN: *Actual size*

7¾ in (20 cm)

Shadow-Quilted Cushion

This is the same basic design as the two trapunto cushions in the preceding project, and also of the Art Nouveau Wall-Hanging on page 134. However, it uses a technique which accommodates the sharp corners without having to turn in a seam allowance.

MATERIALS

36 x 45 in (91.5 x 115 cm) main fabric for cushion (eg, polished cotton)

20 in (51 cm) square organdie or organza

20 in (51 cm) square thin cotton fabric for inside lining of cushion

20 in (51 cm) square thin wadding

¼ yd x 45 in (20 cm x 115 cm) printed cotton

Matching or contrasting quilting thread

18 in (45 cm) square cushion pad

Fusible web such as Bondaweb

EQUIPMENT

Basic sewing kit (needles, pins, scissors, tacking thread, etc)

Template plastic

Trapunto needle

Ruler

Pair of compasses

PREPARING THE DESIGN

1 From the main fabric, cut an 18 in (45 cm) square and two pieces 18 x 12 in (45 x 30 cm).

2 Trace the templates (see page 19) on to plastic and cut out carefully. (DO NOT allow an extra ¼ in (6 mm) all round for turnings as turnings are not needed.) Draw around them on to the fusible web, arranging the shapes close together. Referring to the manufacturers' instructions, bond the web to the printed fabric. Cut out the drawn shapes.

3 Fold and press the fabric to find the centre as shown in Basic Technique (see page 17). Using this point, mark a circle with an 8 in (20 cm) radius. Using the folds and circle as guides, and the diagram of the complete design (see page 65) arrange the bonded shapes onto the background fabric. Bond and press.

QUILTING

4 On a flat surface, place the square of lining fabric, wrong side up, then the wadding, then the main piece (right side up) and last the organdie. Make the quilting 'sandwich' (see Quilting, page 24). Quilt around the applied pieces, close to the edges. The bonding and the quilting stitches will hold the pieces in place.

MAKING UP

5 To make up the cushion cover see Making Cushion Covers, page 32. Insert the cushion pad.

In this technique, the quilting holds the patches in place between the transparent fabric and the background, and the fusible web stops the patches from fraying.

Greetings Cards

*A pack of three or four of these cards would make
an attractive gift, or you can use them to send greetings
to special people.*

MATERIALS

7¾ x 5¾ in (20 x 15 cm) approx card blanks with round apertures

Fabrics with strong repeating patterns

Small amount of thin wadding

Glue stick

EQUIPMENT

Basic sewing kit (needles, pins, scissors, tacking thread, etc)

Template plastic

1   Trace the templates onto plastic and cut out very carefully. Following the instructions in Kaleidoscopes (see page 21) use one of the templates to make a small kaleidoscope. (Because it will be quite small, take great care to do your marking, cutting and stitching very accurately.)

2   Cut a centre from the same fabric or a contrasting one, make up the circle and sew it in place. Press carefully.

3   Open out the card and put glue around the aperture *on the inside of the card*. Place the kaleidoscope, right side up, on the table and hold the open card, right side up over it, making sure that the design is properly centred, and lower the card carefully down on to the kaleidoscope. Press it down with your fingers and turn the card over.

4   Cut a circle from wadding, slightly larger than the aperture, and place it as shown (opposite bottom).

5   Glue and stick down the right-hand side of the card, pressing it hard with your fingers all round. It's a good idea to put the card under a couple of heavy books and leave for a while to make sure it sticks firmly.

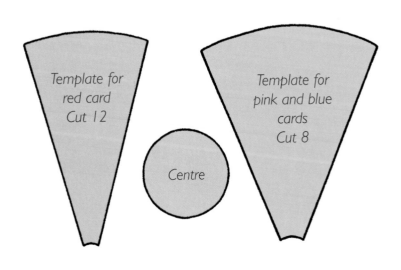

Template for red card
Cut 12

Centre

Template for pink and blue cards
Cut 8

EXAMPLE OF A KALEIDOSCOPE
WITH 8 SEGMENTS

NOTE: Shapes show pattern on
fabric, not appliquéd shapes

Glue here

Glue here

Wadding

Kaleidoscope

Tasselled Tablecloth

There is a slightly heraldic look to this striking cloth, which would look splendid on a circular table, a sofa, or even on a piano. It could be folded in half diagonally and worn as a shawl over a plain dress. While I have specified a blue and gold colour scheme below, of course you don't have to use these colours.

MATERIALS

40 in (102 cm) square of dark blue cotton or polycotton
   (eg polycotton sheeting)
½ yd (46 cm) blue and gold cotton with a strong repeating pattern,
   or a border print
Four or five different blue and gold prints, either scraps or 'fat quarters'
   (see Tip, page 50).
3 skeins stranded gold embroidery thread
Dark blue sewing thread

EQUIPMENT

Basic sewing kit (needles, pins, scissors, tacking thread, etc)
Template plastic
Pair of compasses
Soapstone or chalk pencil
Embroidery needle with a large eye

PREPARING THE DESIGN

1   Turn up a ½ in (12 mm) hem all round the blue square onto the *right* side, and stitch it down with a ¼ in (6 mm) running stitch in the matrallic thread.

2   Fold and press the fabric to find the centre as shown in Basic Technique (see page 17). Also fold and mark the diagonals, to make eight segments.

3   Use your compasses to draw four circles with radii of 6¼, 7¼, 10¼ and 12½ in (16, 18.5, 26 and 32 cm). Mark all these lines with tacking stitches. (This is tedious, but will help you to place the patches accurately on the background.)

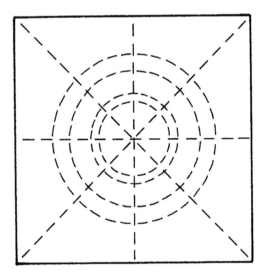

4   Trace the templates onto the template plastic and cut them out carefully.

MAKING THE KALEIDOSCOPE

5   Using the border print and template 2, make a kaleidoscope (see Kaleidoscopes, page 21). Press it and centre it on the background fabric, using your marked lines to place it exactly. Pin, and then sew it down with invisible stitches (see page 18).

6   Stitch circle 1 in the centre of the kaleidoscope, covering the raw edges.

APPLIQUE

7   Cut out the required number of pieces from templates 1, 3, 4, 6, 7, and 8, remembering to allow ¼ in (6 mm) for turnings. Make up the shapes around card (see Marking Circles, Ovals and Other Shapes, page 19), press, remove the card, tack around with small stitches and press again firmly.
Note: the template 5 shape can't be made in this way; just turn in the allowance, tack and press.

8   Lay the cloth on a flat surface and, using the marked lines as a guide, pin and stitch the patches in place, beginning with the template 3 pieces, and working outwards. (See diagram, page 78.)
Note: the circles made from template 6 are sewn together in groups of three before being stitched to the background.

TEMPLATES: *Actual size*

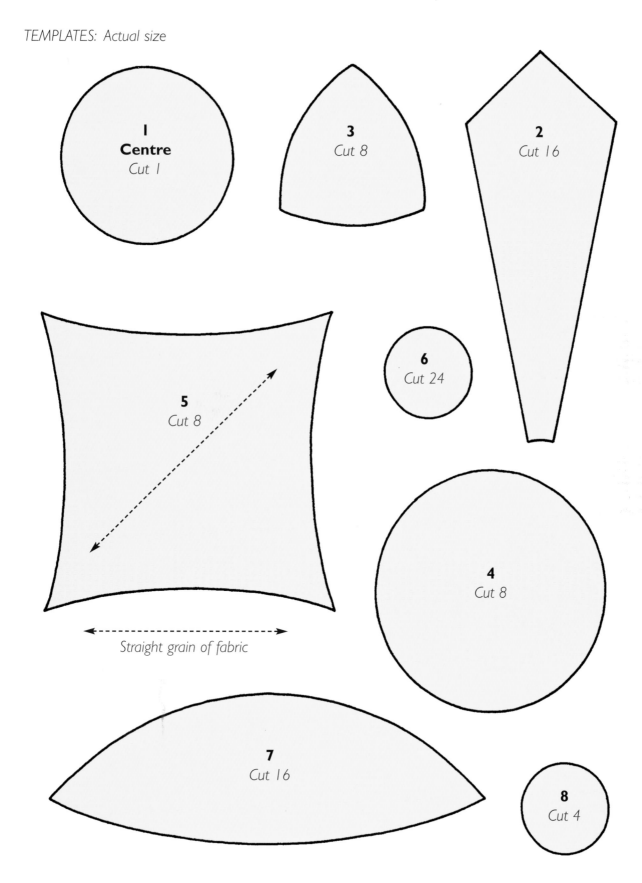

I
Centre
Cut 1

3
Cut 8

2
Cut 16

5
Cut 8

6
Cut 24

4
Cut 8

Straight grain of fabric

7
Cut 16

8
Cut 4

9 When all the pieces are sewn on, press the cloth and then sew a row of ¼ in (6 mm) running stitches in the gold thread just outside the outer circle.

TASSELS

10 Make four tassels as follows: cut two pieces of stiff card 3½ x 4½ in (9 x 11.5 cm). Wind the gold thread round the two pieces of card about 25 times (below).

QUARTER OF DESIGN: 50% actual size

12½ in (32 cm)

11 Thread the embroidery needle with about 8 in (20 cm) of gold thread. Push the needle under the top of the wound thread and tie the ends together very securely (below). Slip your scissors between the two pieces of a card at the bottom of the wound thread and cut through all the threads.

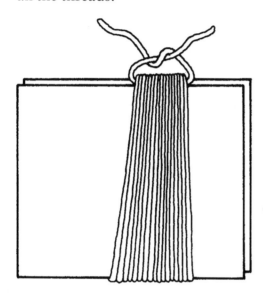

TIP
Thread length
   Don't have your thread too long when doing any kind of stitching. It will wear through, or become tangled, or tie itself around your pins. If it still twists itself around the pins, try using very small pins or, instead of pinning, tack your pieces to the background with fairly small stitches before finally stitching the patches down.

12 To make the head of the tassel, bind it about ½ in (12 mm) from the top, winding the thread round about ten times and secure by stitching through the binding several times. Sew one tassel to each corner of the cloth and cover the stitches with the circles made from template 8.

The contrasting tassells give this cloth a decorative three-dimensional finishing touch.

Kaleidoscope Footstool

*Another accessory using the kaleidoscope technique,
this little footstool looks too pretty to put your feet on.
This design may be easily adapted for use on a square footstool,
which could be made at home more simply than a round stool,
avoiding the expense of a purchased one.*

MATERIALS

Purchased round footstool, 11 inches (28 cm) approx in diameter
18 inch (46 cm) square of black cotton fabric for background
1/2yd (0.5 m) approx cotton fabric with repeat or border print
Small scrap of contrast fabric
60 in (1.6 m) 1/4 in (6 mm) wide black iron-on bias tape

EQUIPMENT

Basic sewing kit (needles, pins, scissors, tacking thread, etc)
Template plastic
Soapstone or chalk pencil

1   Fold and press the fabric to find the centre as shown in Basic Technique (see page 17). Also fold and mark the diagonals, to make eight segments.

2   Trace the templates onto the template plastic and cut them out carefully.

3   Using template 1 and the border print, make a kaleidoscope (see Kaleidoscopes, page 21). Cover the seams with bias tape, first pressing it on and then stitching it down, tucking the ends under the outer edge of the kaleidoscope.

4   Using template 2, make a circle from the contrasting fabric and apply it to the centre.

5   Using the marking on the background fabric as a guide, apply the kaleidoscope, pin and then sew it down with invisible stitches (see page 18).

6   Cut eight pieces from template 3 and eight more from template 4 using selected, matching parts of the border print. Make up the shapes (see Making Circles Ovals and Other Shapes, page 19). Stitch these pieces on the background as shown in the diagram (opposite).

MAKING UP
7   This project doesn't need to be quilted so you can now go ahead and make up the footstool according to the manufacturer's instructions.

TEMPLATES: *Actual size*

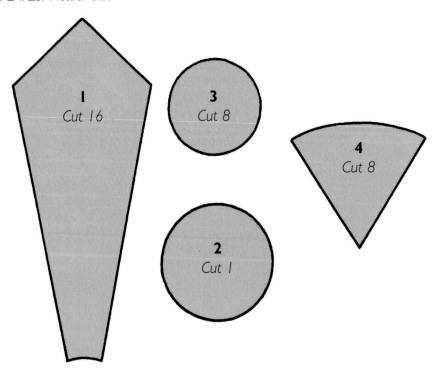

1 Cut 16

3 Cut 8

4 Cut 8

2 Cut 1

QUARTER OF DESIGN: *Actual size*

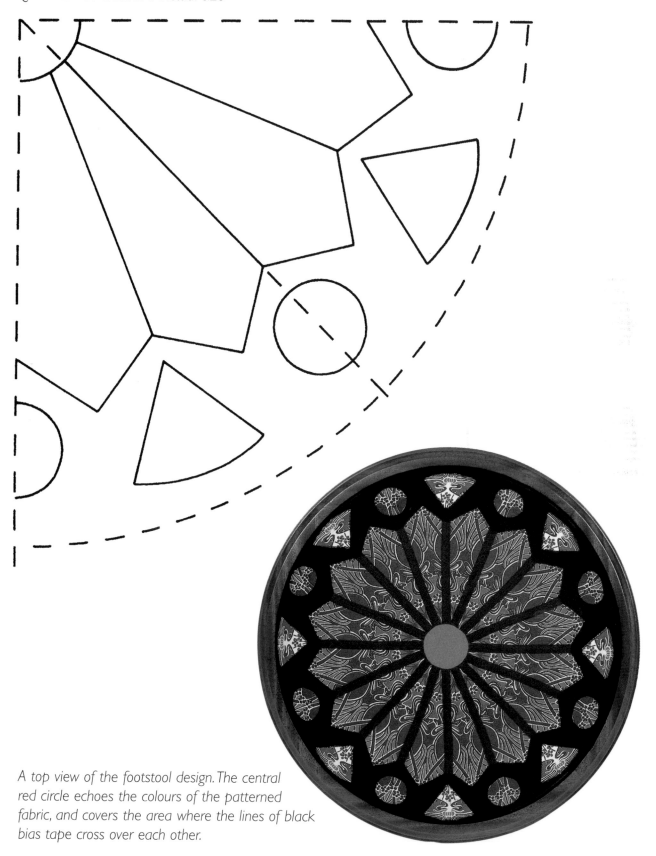

A top view of the footstool design. The central red circle echoes the colours of the patterned fabric, and covers the area where the lines of black bias tape cross over each other.

Liberty Fans

*This little wall-hanging wasn't intended to be a rose-window quilt
but was my first experiment with repeating designs
used to make a simple kaleidoscope pattern.
However, when I have it with me while demonstrating
at a quilt show it seems to attract a lot of attention,
so I'm including it here.*

MATERIALS

Three different Liberty fabrics were used in this example, but you could try it
with just one. You should be able to cut 12 different half circles
of fans from $\frac{1}{2}$ yd (0.5m) of fabric, so you will have to decide how much
to buy, depending on how many fabrics you want to use, and what size
hanging you want to make. This one is 26 in (66 cm) square.

1 yd (1 m) of background fabric

Small amount contrasting fabric for binding

27 in (70 cm) square thin wadding.

27 in (70 cm square backing fabric

Quilting thread to match patterned fabric and background

EQUIPMENT

Basic sewing kit (needles, pins, scissors, tacking thread, etc)

Template plastic

A.M.B.   1994.

1   From the background fabric cut 21 pieces: one 8½ in (21.5 cm) square, twelve pieces 4½ x 8½ in (11.5 x 21.5 cm) and eight 4½ in (11.5 cm) squares.

2   Trace the templates onto the template plastic and cut them out carefully.

3   Using template 1 and the repeat-patterned fabric, and following instructions given in Kaleidoscopes, page 21, make one full circle with 16 segments (for the central panel), 12 half circles (8 segments) and eight quarter circles (4 segments). Remember to add ¼ in (6 mm) onto each fabric piece for turnings.

4   Apply the kaleidoscopes to the background fabric pieces and cover the open middles with a circle for the centre, and either a half or quarter circle cut from the same or contrasting fabrics (templates 2, 3 and 4).

5   Join the blocks as shown opposite. Quilt around the outside of the kaleidoscopes, the centre circle, the half circles and quarter circles and 'in the ditch' around each block (see Quilting, page 25).

6   Finally, bind the quilt, sew on either a sleeve or loops for hanging (see Hanging a Quilt, page 30) and hang it in a conspicuous place to be admired by all.

TEMPLATES: *Actual size*

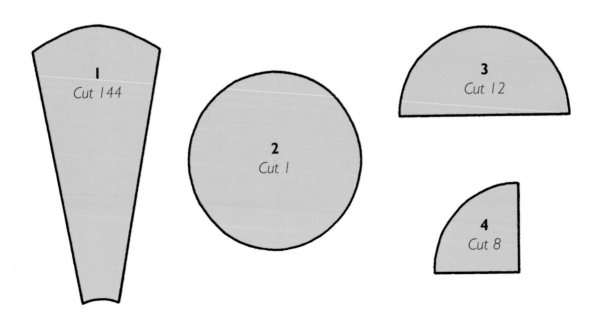

1
Cut 144

2
Cut 1

3
Cut 12

4
Cut 8

DESIGN OF QUILT: *To scale*

'Oranges and Lemons' Tablecloth and Napkins

Buy or make a round tablecloth and eight napkins
and use them in the garden on hot sunny days.
Pale yellow polycotton sheeting was used for this example.
It is very wide and comes in a good selection of colours.
The co-ordinating 'orange and lemon' fabrics
were already in my fabric collection
(I knew they would come in useful one day)
but floral prints or any other theme would work equally well.

MATERIALS FOR TABLECLOTH AND EIGHT NAPKINS

1½ yd (1.4 m) polycotton sheeting

Patterned fabric

Matching thread

Binding: I made bias binding and bound the cloth and the napkins
as I had plenty of fabric, but purchased binding may be used, or
the items need not be bound at all.

EQUIPMENT

Basic sewing kit (needles, pins, scissors, tacking thread, etc)

Template plastic

Tablecloth

TEMPLATES: *Actual size*

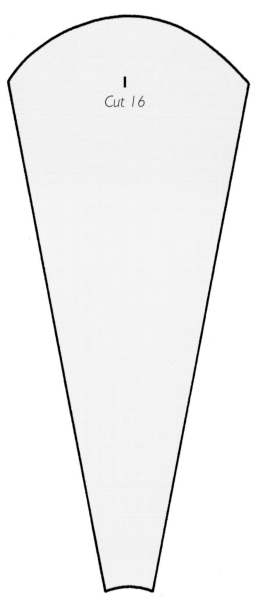

PREPARING THE DESIGN

1 To make the circle, fold background fabric in half and then in half again into quarters. Make an arc 25 in (63.5 cm) from the corner: a pin with a piece of string tied to it, and a pencil tied to the other end will make an accurate curve; or swing a ruler with a pencil or marker. Cut along the line.

2 Turn up a ½ in (12 mm) hem all round onto the *wrong* side, or bind the edge with bought or your own bias binding.

3 Divide the cloth into eight segments (see page 40) and draw circles with radii of 7 and 11 in (18 and 28 cm). (You could make the design larger by adding further rings of shapes to the cloth.) Mark all these lines with tacking stitches. (This is tedious, but will help you to place the patches accurately.)

MAKING THE CENTRE CIRCLE

4 Using the patterned fabric and template 1, make a central circle (see Kaleidoscopes, page 21). It is not a true kaleidoscope as the pieces are not cut from a matching part of the fabric pattern. Press it and centre it carefully on the background, using your marked lines to place it exactly. Pin, and then sew with invisible stitches (see page 18).

APPLIQUE

5 Cut out the required number of pieces from templates 2, 3 and 4, remembering to allow ¼ in (6 mm) for turnings. Make up the shapes around card (see Marking Circles, Ovals and Other Shapes, page 20), press, remove the card, tack around with small stitches and press again firmly.

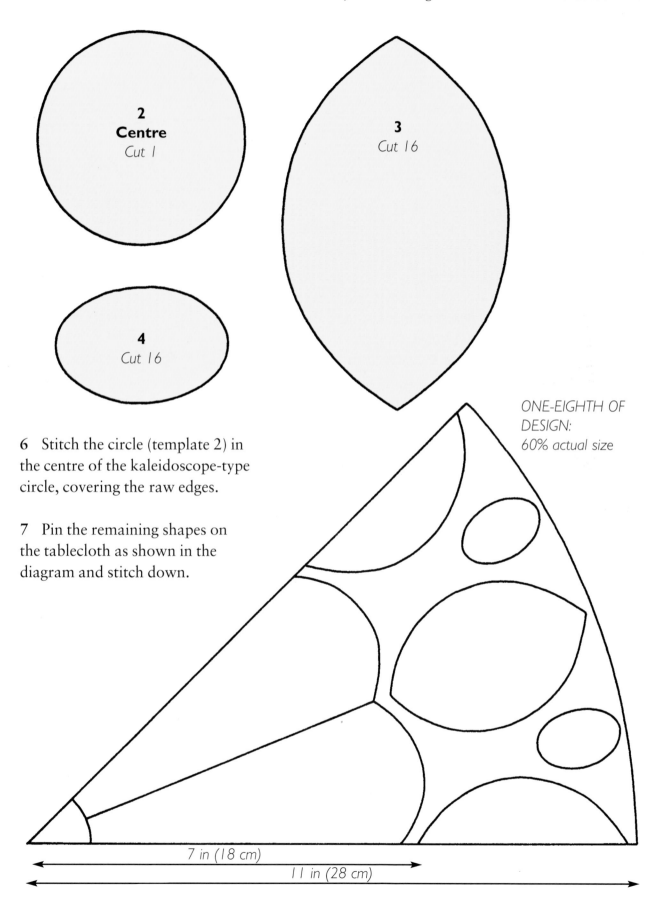

2
Centre
Cut 1

3
Cut 16

4
Cut 16

6 Stitch the circle (template 2) in the centre of the kaleidoscope-type circle, covering the raw edges.

7 Pin the remaining shapes on the tablecloth as shown in the diagram and stitch down.

ONE-EIGHTH OF DESIGN:
60% actual size

7 in (18 cm)
11 in (28 cm)

Napkins

Each napkin has two segments of a 16-segment circle and when the napkins are folded into eight and laid in a circle, a small rose window appears. A gimmick, perhaps, but amusing.

1 Cut eight circles of fabric with a radius of 8 in (20 cm). Hem or bind the edges as for the tablecloth.

2 Divide each napkin into eight segments (see page 40) and draw a circle with a radius of 4½ in (11.5 cm). Mark one segment.

3 Using the patterned fabric and templates 1N and 2N, cut out the required number of pieces, remembering to add on ¼ in (6 mm) all round for turnings.

4 For each napkin, join two 1N pieces together down one long side, as if you were making a kaleidoscope (see page 21). Turn the edges in, tack around with small stitches and press again firmly.

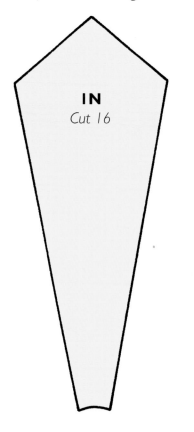

1N
Cut 16

2N
Cut 8

NAPKIN TEMPLATES: *Actual size*

NAPKIN SHAPES: Joined together

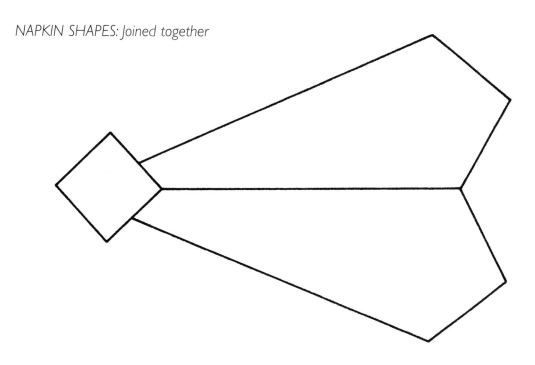

5   Pin the two joined pieces on to the marked segment of each napkin and stitch down. Cover the centre raw edge with the square 2N and stitch down.

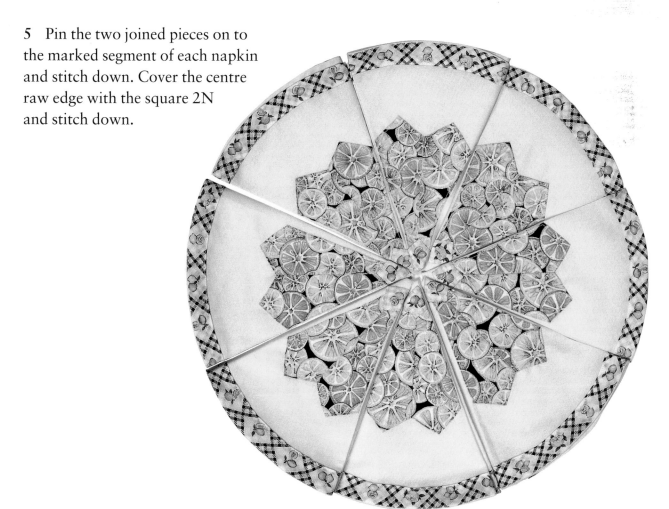

Sarah's Quilt

*This bright little wall-hanging was made as a commission,
a gift for a young woman's twenty-first birthday.
She had seen my work at a quilt show and was, apparently,
impressed. Her mother worte to ask if I would make a quilt
for the forthcoming birthday and I agreed,
on the condition that I could use it in this book.
I was quite sorry when the quilt went to its new home
as it turned out to be one of my favourite pieces.*

MATERIALS

26 in (66 cm) square black cotton for background

26 in (66 cm) square cotton for backing

26 in (66 cm) square wadding

Brightly coloured fabrics for patches

3 yd (3 m) x ¼ in (6 mm) black iron-on bias tape

Heavy interlining (for all coloured shapes except big segmented circle)

EQUIPMENT

Basic sewing kit (needles, pins, scissors, tacking thread, etc)

Template plastic

Soapstone or chalk pencil

PREPARING THE DESIGN

1   Divide the square of black cotton background fabric into 16 segments (22.5° each) as described in Basic Technique, page 17. Mark two circles with radii of 7½ and 11 in (19 and 28 cm), to help with placement of patches.

TEMPLATES: Actual size

2   Make plastic templates, tracing them from the template diagram.

MAKING THE CENTRE CIRCLE

3   Using the patterned fabric and template 1, (remembering to add ¼ in (6 mm) for turnings) make a circle in the same way as a kaleidoscope: see Kaleidoscopes, page 21. (It is not a true kaleidoscope as the pieces are not cut from a matching part of the fabric pattern.) Press the circle and centre it on the background, using the marked lines to place it exactly. Pin, and then sew with invisible stitches. Cover the seams with the bias tape.

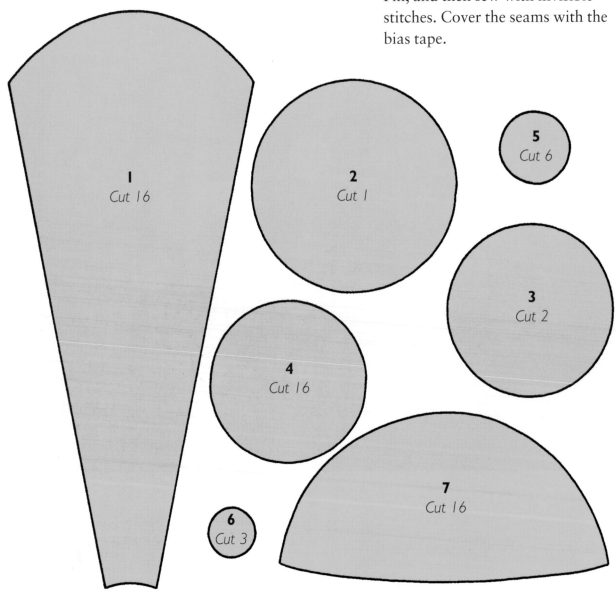

1
Cut 16

2
Cut 1

5
Cut 6

3
Cut 2

4
Cut 16

6
Cut 3

7
Cut 16

4 Draw templates 2, 3, 4, 5, 6 and 7 straight onto interfacing. (These may be left inside the finished piece.) Cut out carefully.

5 Cut out the patches from the patterned fabric, remembering to add ¼ in (6 mm) for turnings.

APPLIQUE AND QUILTING

6 Make up the shapes with interlining as shown in Making Circles, Ovals and Other Shapes, page 20. The template 5 circles are joined in groups of four before being applied to the background (see below).

7 Use circles 2 and 3 to cover the centre of the circle.

8 Arrange pieces 4, 5, 6 and 7 on the background and stitch in place. Press.

9 Make the quilting 'sandwich' (see Quilting, page 24) and quilt around each patch.

MAKING UP

10 Make the binding from some contrasting fabric (see Binding a Quilt, page 31). Add a sleeve for a hanging rod (see Hanging a Quilt, page 30).

ONE-EIGHTH OF DESIGN: 60% actual size

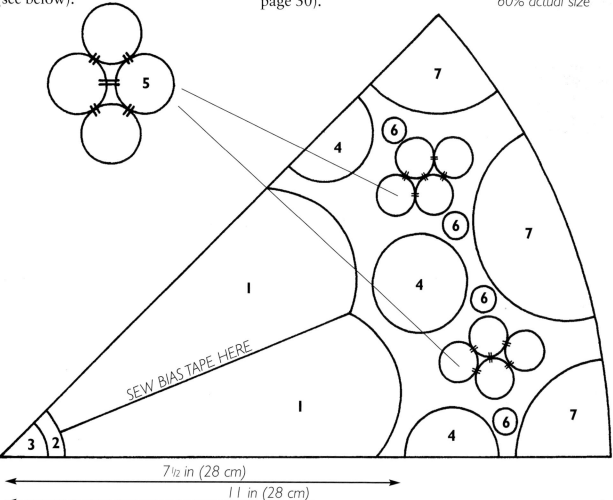

7½ in (28 cm)

11 in (28 cm)

'Strasbourg' Wall-Hanging

This hanging was made several years ago for a fiftieth wedding anniversary gift for good friends, who have kindly lent it to me to use in this section of the book. It is based on the centre part of a rose window in Strasbourg cathedral.

MATERIALS

2 x 28 in (71 cm) squares black cotton, for background and backing

28 in (71 cm) square wadding

Brightly coloured fabrics for patches

EQUIPMENT

Basic sewing kit (needles, pins, scissors, tacking thread, etc)

Template plastic

Soapstone or chalk pencil

1   Divide the square of black cotton background fabric into 12 segments (30° each) as described in Basic Technique, page 17. Mark two circles with radii of 8½ and 12 in (21.5 and 30.5 cm), to help with placement of patches.

2   Make plastic templates, tracing them from the template diagram. Cut the shapes from the patterned fabrics, adding ¼ in (6 mm) all round for turnings.

3   Make up the shapes without interlining as shown in Making Circles, Ovals and Other Shapes, page 20. Units A and B should be assembled before applying them to the background.

4   Arrange all the pieces on the background and stitch in place. Press.

5   Make the quilting 'sandwich' (see Quilting, page 24) and quilt around each patch.

MAKING UP

6   Make the binding from background fabric (see Binding a Quilt, page 31). Add a sleeve for a hanging rod (see Hanging a Quilt, page 30).

QUARTER OF DESIGN:
50% actual size

TEMPLATES:
Actual size

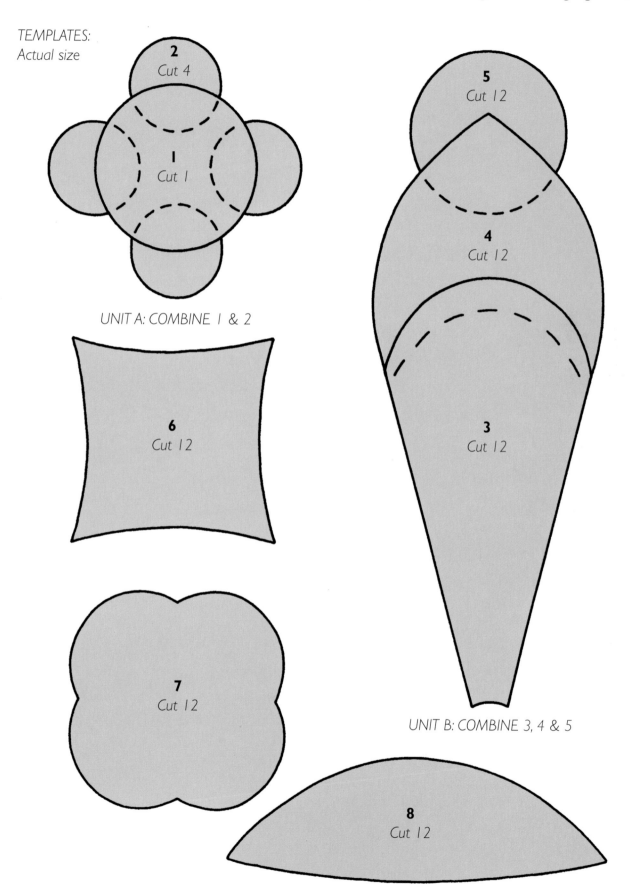

2
Cut 4

1
Cut 1

UNIT A: COMBINE 1 & 2

5
Cut 12

4
Cut 12

3
Cut 12

6
Cut 12

7
Cut 12

UNIT B: COMBINE 3, 4 & 5

8
Cut 12

'Washington' Wall-Hanging

*This wall-hanging is based on one of the rose windows in the
National Cathedral in Washington DC.
More than eighty different fabrics were used in it,
so it's a good project for using scraps.
It lives on one of the walls in my sitting-room and
makes a good talking point.
Collect as many bright fabrics as you can find for the patches,
although it could be interesting to make all of them
in the same fabric.*

MATERIALS

2 x 54 in (137 cm) squares black cotton, for background and backing

54 in (137 cm) square wadding

Brightly coloured fabrics for patches

Heavy interlining (for small circles)

EQUIPMENT

Basic sewing kit (needles, pins, scissors, tacking thread, etc)

Template plastic

Soapstone or chalk pencil

1 Find the centre of the fabric and draw a circle with a 24 in (61 cm) radius and divide it into 20 segments (18° each) as described in Basic Technique, page 17. Mark two circles with radii of 9 and 15½ in (23 and 39.5 cm), to help with placement of patches.

2 Make plastic templates, tracing them from the template diagram. Cut the shapes from the patterned fabrics, adding ¼ in (6 mm) all round for turnings.

TEMPLATES:
Actual size

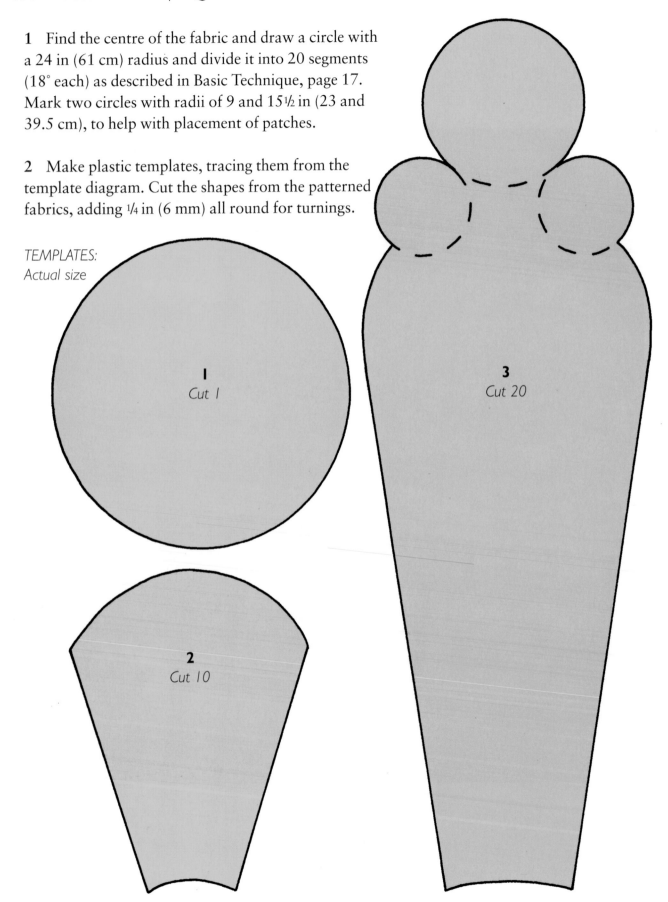

1
Cut 1

2
Cut 10

3
Cut 20

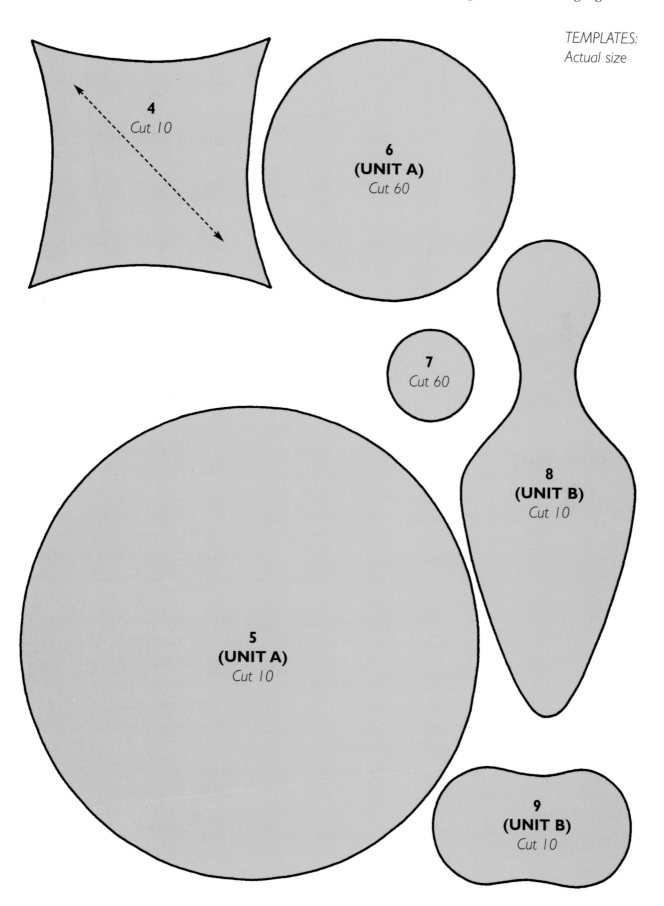

4
Cut 10

6
(UNIT A)
Cut 60

7
Cut 60

5
(UNIT A)
Cut 10

8
(UNIT B)
Cut 10

9
(UNIT B)
Cut 10

TEMPLATES: Actual size

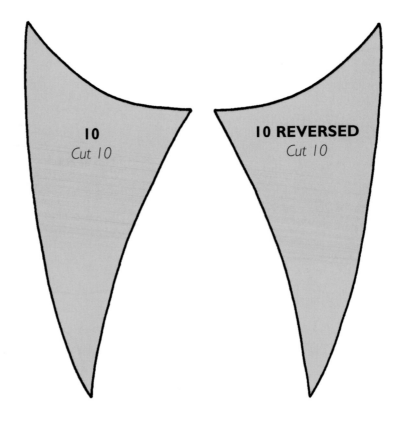

10
Cut 10

10 REVERSED
Cut 10

3 Using the patterned fabric and shape 2, make a kaleidoscope (see Kaleidoscopes, page 21). Press it and centre it on the background, using the marks to place it exactly. Pin, and then sew with invisible stitches. Sew circle 1 in the centre.

4 Take the 20 shape-3 pieces and stitch in place, one in each segment.

5 Sew shape-5 patches between alternate shape-3 pieces.

6 Make up 10 each of Units A (shapes 5 and 6) and B (shapes 8 and 9), and apply them.

7 Make 60 small circles from shape 7, using the Shapes with Interlining method (see page 20).

Leave the interlining inside the finished pieces. Sew six around each Unit A.

8 Cut ten patches each from templates 10 and 10 Reversed and sew them around the outer circle.

9 Make the quilting 'sandwich' and quilt just outside the patches and around the outer circle. If you wish, you could also use Vermicelli quilting in the corners of the quilt. (See Quilting, page 24.)

MAKING UP
6 Make the binding from background fabric (see Binding a Quilt, page 31). Add a sleeve for a hanging rod (see Hanging a Quilt, page 30).

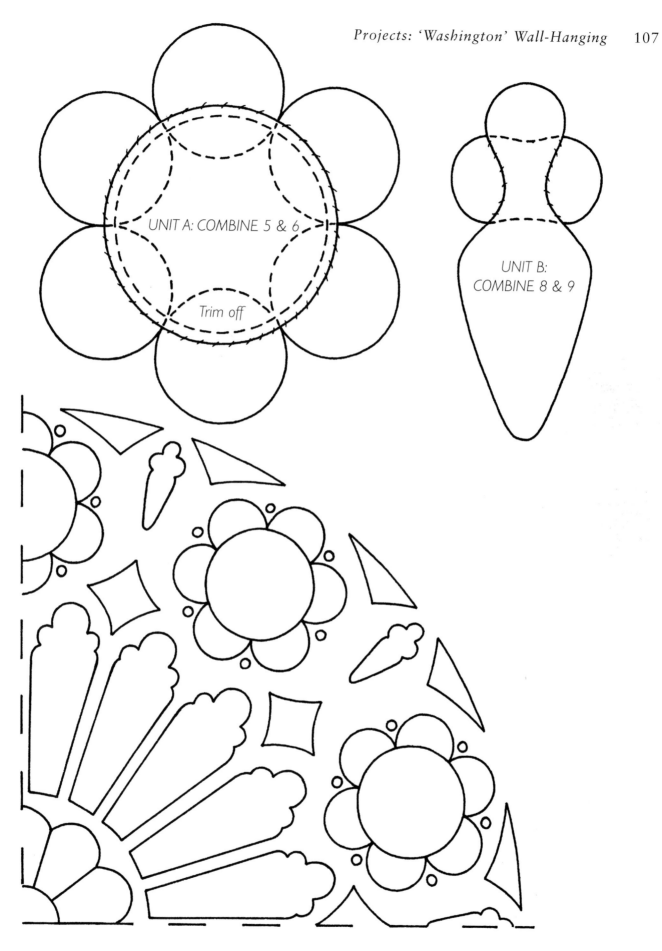

UNIT A: COMBINE 5 & 6

Trim off

UNIT B:
COMBINE 8 & 9

'Chartres' Wall-Hanging

The last of my projects is the first rose-window quilt
I ever made, the one which started it all,
about which I wrote in the Introduction (see page 7).

MATERIALS

Two 58 x 48 in (147 x 122 cm) rectangles black cotton, for background
    and backing
46 x 56 in (117 x 142 cm) rectangle of wadding
Brightly coloured fabrics for patches
9½ yd (9 m) x ¼ in (6 mm) black iron-on bias tape

EQUIPMENT

Basic sewing kit (needles, pins, scissors, tacking thread, etc)
Template plastic
Soapstone or chalk pencil

PREPARING THE DESIGN

1 Find the centre of the fabric and draw a circle with an 18 in (46 cm) radius. Divide the circle into 12 segments (30° each) as described in Basic Technique, page 17. Then mark a circle with a radius of 10½ in (26.5 cm), to help with placement of patches.

2 Make plastic templates, tracing them from the template diagram. Cut the shapes from the patterned fabrics, adding ¼ in (6 mm) all round for turnings.

3 Using the patterned fabric and shapes 2 and 3, make two circles in the same way as a kaleidoscope (see Kaleidoscopes, page 21). (They are not true kaleidoscopes as the pieces are not cut from a matching part of the fabric pattern.) Press both and centre on the background, using the marked lines to place them exactly. Pin, and then sew with invisible stitches. Sew bias tape over each seam of the circle.

4 Sew circle 1 in the centre of the smaller kaleidoscope/circle.

5 Apply 12 of shape 4, placing bias tape on the lines indicated, and covering the centre of each shape with a shape 5. (See diagram of complete quilt on page 114.)

TEMPLATES: Actual size

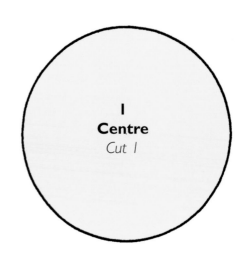

I
Centre
Cut I

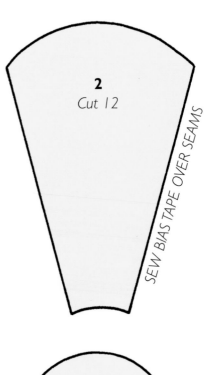

2
Cut I2

SEW BIAS TAPE OVER SEAMS

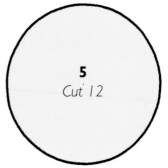

5
Cut I2

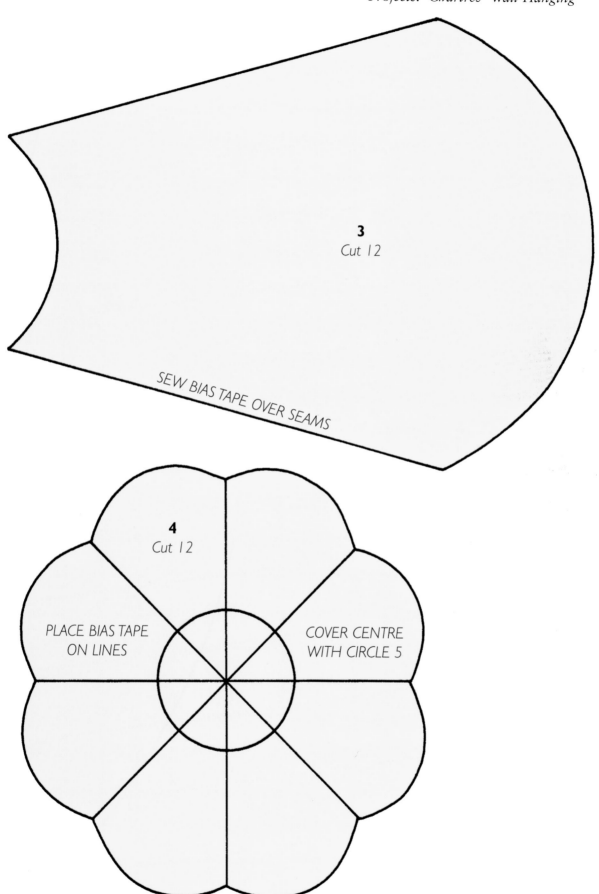

3
Cut 12

SEW BIAS TAPE OVER SEAMS

4
Cut 12

PLACE BIAS TAPE
ON LINES

COVER CENTRE
WITH CIRCLE 5

6   Unit A is made by making four of shape 6, and then sewing them together (below).

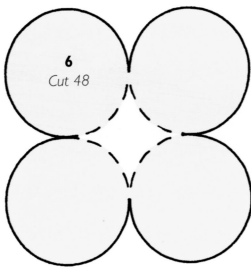

6
Cut 48

7   Add the shape-7 pieces, placing them around the outer circle.

8   Place the shape-8 pieces at the top and bottom of the rose, spacing them evenly.

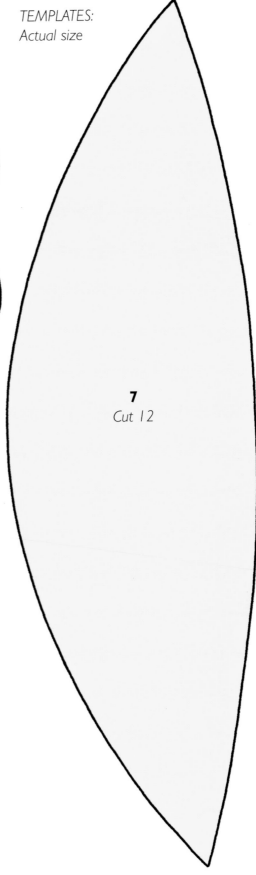

7
Cut 12

9 Make the quilting 'sandwich' and quilt just outside the patches and around the outer circle. (See Quilting, page 24.)

MAKING UP

10 Bind the quilt by trimming the backing and wadding so that they are 1 in (2.5 cm) smaller on each side than the background fabric. (The finished quilt measures 46 x 56 in (117 x 142 cm.) Take the background to the back so that the binding does not show at the front, rather than the usual way of bringing the backing to the front (see Binding a Quilt, page 31).

11 Make a sleeve to hang the quilt (see Hanging a Quilt, page 30).

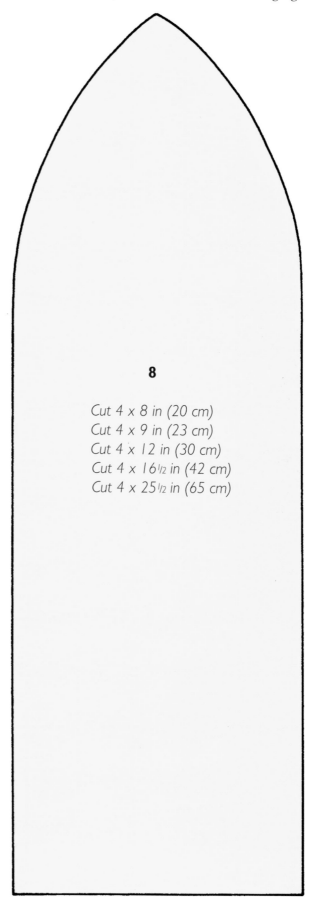

8

Cut 4 x 8 in (20 cm)
Cut 4 x 9 in (23 cm)
Cut 4 x 12 in (30 cm)
Cut 4 x 16½ in (42 cm)
Cut 4 x 25½ in (65 cm)

'GUEST' ARTISTES

The final section of this book features the work of three people who have each given some of their precious time to making a project for me to include.

◀ I have known *Gail Lawther* for a long time: hardly surprising, as she is my daughter. Gail's sofa throw is typical of her work, which uses exotic fabrics and beautiful machine appliqué.

▶ *Persis Darling* and I met about nine years ago, at a fair called Quilting-by-the-Lake in New York state. She lives in Maryland, USA, and we now meet once a year, to attend a quilt show either in Europe or America. The Christmas Tree skirt made by Persis is, to my mind, typically American, while still using the rose-window format.

She also made the St Eustache rose-window quilt featured in the Introduction on page 6.

◀ *Barbara Furse* is one of my newer friends, one of the many whom I have met in the five or so years since I returned from Italy to live in England. Barbara's wall-hanging – which uses the same design as the various cushions on pages 62–70 – demonstrates her meticulous appliqué.

Monochrome Sofa Throw

❖ *Gail Lawther* ❖

Try something a little bit different with this glittery sofa throw, which uses sheeny and metallic fabrics in greys and silvers. The pieces are appliquéd using machine satin stitch, which allows you to create the lovely curved points of the petal shapes easily and avoids any need for turning and neatening the edges of the fabric pieces.

MATERIALS

44 x 24 in (112 x 61 cm) firm black foundation fabric.
   (To set off the appliqué pieces, try to find a fabric with a slight sheen.)
48 x 28 in (122 x 71cm) black for the backing and binding.
   (Choose one with a slight pattern woven into it, such as brocade or damask.)
44 x 24 in (112 x 61 cm) 2 oz (50 g) polyester wadding

continued on page 118

MATERIALS, CONTINUED

Nine different metallic and shiny fabrics in silvers and greys:

Fabric 1: 20 in (51 cm) square: used for 8 template-A shapes

Fabric 2: 20 in (51 cm) square: used for 8 template-A shapes

Fabric 3: 20 x 16 in (51 x 41 cm): used for the wing shapes that create the main circle design

Fabric 4: 16 x 6 in (41 x 15 cm): used for the duck-feet shapes between the wings

Fabric 5: 12 x 6 in (30 x 15 cm): used for the curved triangles at the corners

Fabric 6: Large scrap: used for the almond shapes

Fabric 7: 9 in (23 cm) square: used for the large kite shapes down the middle of the design

Fabric 8: 6 x 3 in (15 x 7.5 cm): used for the central circles

Fabric 9: 10 x 6 in (25.5 x 15 cm): used for the curved triangles at centre top and bottom

Try to choose fabrics in a selection of tones, from light silver to dark charcoal.

If any of your chosen fabrics have strong patterns that you want to keep in the same direction on all the pieces, you will need more of those fabrics.

2 yd (2 m) x 18 in (46 cm) wide lightweight Bondaweb or Heat 'n' Bond

44 x 24 in (112 x 61 cm) Stitch 'n' Tear or similar tear-away foundation

1000 m reel Madeira black rayon machine embroidery thread

Black sewing thread

Black quilting thread (optional)

EQUIPMENT

Basic sewing kit (needles, pins, scissors, tacking thread, etc)

Chalk or soapstone marker

Pencil

Quilting needle (optional)

PREPARING THE DESIGN

1 Press all the fabrics. As metallics can melt or pucker easily, use the minimum iron heat necessary and, where possible, press the fabrics from the back. (A damp cloth between the iron and the fabric can also be useful if the fabric tends to stick. Always try pressing a little sample of each fabric first.)

2 Using a pencil, trace the templates onto the paper side of the Bondaweb or Heat 'n' Bond in the quantities listed. Do all the tracings of template A first, fitting the shapes into each other to make the most of the fusible web and just leaving a small margin around each shape, then continue with templates B, C, D, E, etc.

TEMPLATES: *Actual size*

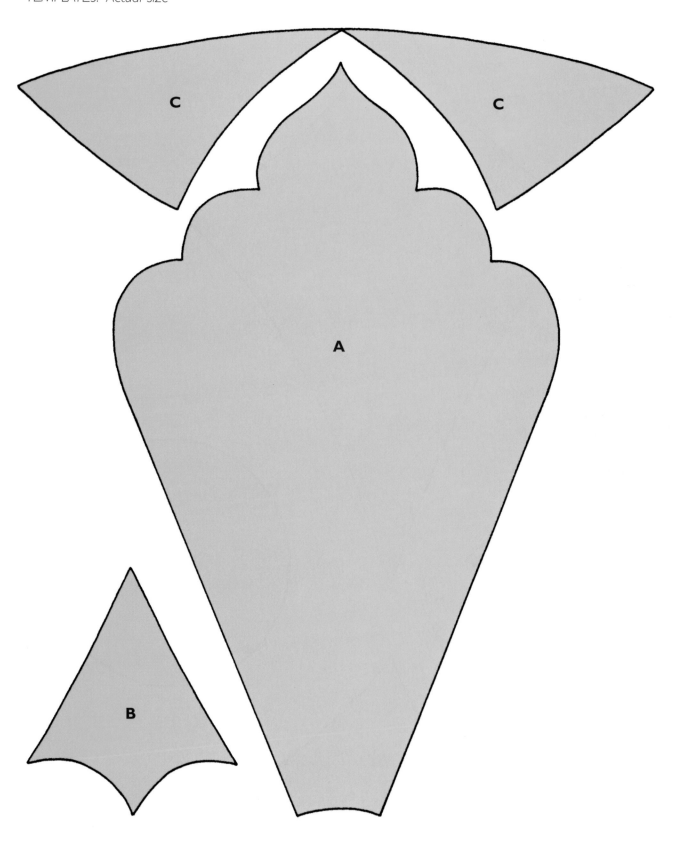

TEMPLATES: Actual size

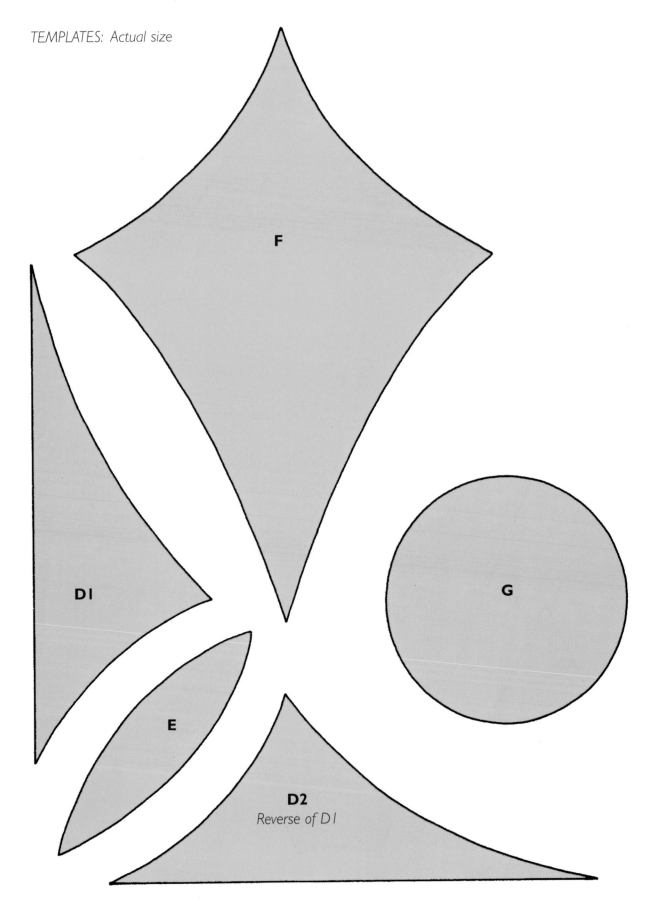

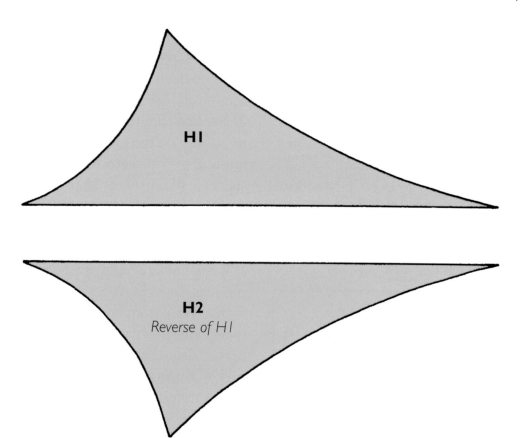

H1

H2
Reverse of H1

3   Fabric 1 is used for eight of the template-A shapes. If the pattern direction isn't important for this particular fabric, you can fuse the fusible web tracings onto the back of the fabric as a whole piece, without cutting each individual shape out. Lay the fabric face down on the ironing board, position the fusible web web-side down on the back, and fuse it into place with a warm iron.

   If the pattern is important, cut out each of the eight tracings individually, leaving a small margin outside the lines, then position the shapes on the back of the fabric so that the pattern is in the same direction on each one. Fuse them on in the same way.

4   Continue in this way using the following fabrics and template shapes:

   Fabric 2: 8 template A
   Fabric 3: 16 template C
   Fabric 4: 16 template B
   Fabric 5: 4 template D1,
             4 template D2
   Fabric 6: 8 template E
   Fabric 7: 2 template F
   Fabric 8: 2 template G
   Fabric 9: 2 template H1,
             2 template H2

5   Cut all the shapes out along the pencil lines. (You may find it helpful to have a series of small plastic bags or envelopes to put the shapes in as you cut them, so that you don't lose track of any of them.)

6 Mark the centre lines of the foundation fabric horizontally and vertically in chalk or soapstone marker. Measure out 10 in (25 cm) from the vertical centre line at the top edge, middle and bottom edge of the fabric, and use these measurements to draw in two more vertical lines (below). These lines will help you to position the main circles of the design.

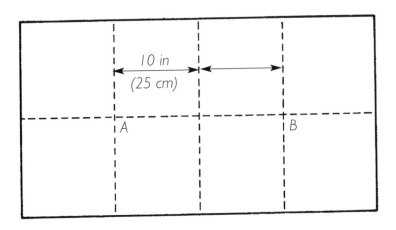

7 Using points A and B as the centres, draw in circles of 9½ in (24cm) radius (see Basic Techniques, page 17). Then draw in the 45° lines on these circles (opposite top).

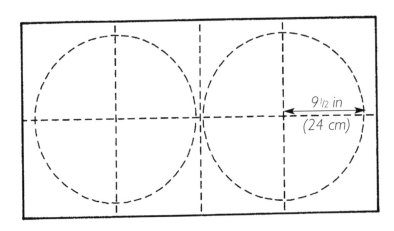

8 Peel the backing papers off all the template-A shapes, and position them inside the circles (opposite). Alternate fabrics 1 and 2, and line each template up so that its point is on the relevant marker line and so that there are even spaces between all the shapes. Peel the papers off the two central circles (template G) and put them in position.

When you are happy with the placings, fuse the pieces in position with a warm iron, being careful not to dislodge them as you fuse. If any of the fabrics have a tendency to stick to the iron, lay a clean damp cloth carefully over the shapes when they are in position and then iron over the cloth.

9 Add the wing shapes (template C) and the duck-foot shapes (template B) around each circle in the same way (opposite), keeping the outside line of the circles smooth and the spaces between shapes even.

10 Use the chalk or soapstone marker and a long ruler to draw a rectangle touching the sides of the circles (opposite). Use these lines to position the cornerpieces and the central sections of the design (see page 124).

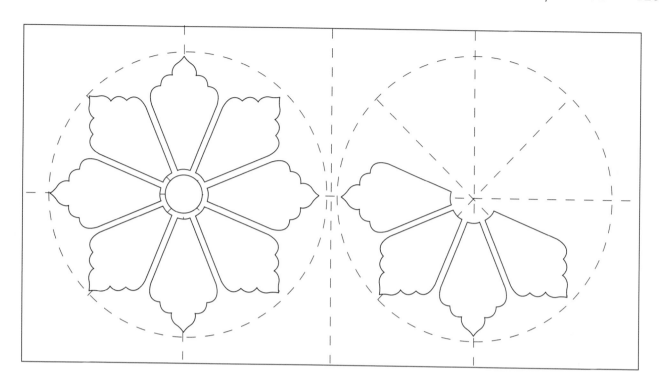

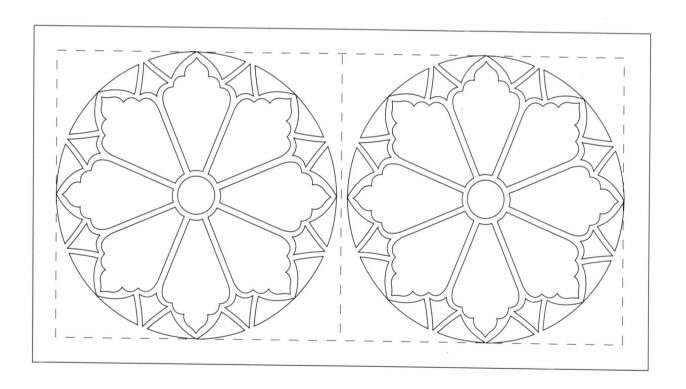

11 Lay the tear-away backing on a flat surface and cover with the wadding, then lay the appliqué fabric, right side up, on top. Make a quilting 'sandwich' (see Quilting, page 24) by tacking the three layers together, but tack around and between the shapes rather than across them: this will make it much easier to remove the tacking stitches afterwards, as they won't be caught up in the machine stitching.

12 Set your sewing machine for satin stitch, ⅛ in (4 mm) wide, and thread the top needle with the Madeira thread, and the bobbin with ordinary black sewing thread. If your bobbin case has a tiny hole in the end of its arm, put the thread through that before you put it into the machine; this helps to produce a firm, even stitch.

13 Stitch all the way around the large marked circles first, keeping the curve even and catching down the outside edges of the wing shapes as you go. When you come to the end of a stitching line, put the stitch width to '0' and work a couple of stitches on top of each other to finish off the thread neatly.

14 In the same way, stitch round the central circles, again keeping the curves smooth. Now stitch round the main petal shapes, narrowing the stitches when you come to the tip of each shape to make a satisfying point. Stitch all the duck-foot shapes, then stitch round the curved inner edges of the wing shapes – you should be able to do all the wing shapes round each circle without having to stop and start the stitching. Finally, stitch round all the triangles, almond shapes and kite shapes that make up the corner pieces and central decorations.

15 Remove the tacking stitches, and pull away all the backing paper from outside and within the stitched shapes.

16 Lay the backing fabric, right side down, on a flat surface and lay the quilted panel, right side up, on top so that there is an even border of backing fabric all round the edge. Tack or pin the layers together at even intervals, then add quilted lines by hand or machine: just stitch around the main pattern pieces, as here, or you could fill the whole border with a decorative stitch. Remove the tacking.

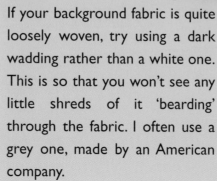

TIP
Using coloured wadding
If your background fabric is quite loosely woven, try using a dark wadding rather than a white one. This is so that you won't see any little shreds of it 'bearding' through the fabric. I often use a grey one, made by an American company.

17 Fold each edge of the backing fabric over to the front in a double fold to create an even border: fold the corners straight across, or mitre them if you prefer. Then stitch the edges of the fold down by hand, or using a machine to complete the sofa throw.

Christmas Tree Skirt

❖ *Persis Darling* ❖

*A beautifully decorative cover to hide the base of a Christmas tree.
It seems a pity to cover it up with presents,
but it comes into its own after all the gifts have been opened.*

MATERIALS

Fabric – all quantities based on 44–45 in
  (112–115 cm) wide fabric
1¼ yd (1.2 m) for background
1½ yd (1.4 m) for backing
1½ yd (1.4 m) flannelette or very thin wadding

First Ring: Father Christmases
½ yd (45 cm) green
½ yd (45 cm) red
⅛ yd (12 cm) flesh colour
Scraps of white

Second Ring: Teardrop Balls
(This fabric also used for the border)
1¼ yd (1.2 m) bright Christmas fabric

Third Ring: Trees
½ yd (45 cm) green (If using green for
  background, use a different green for
  the trees)
Scraps of brown for trunks

Border
Use the same fabric as for the teardrop
  balls

Other materials
Decorative threads and threads to match
fabrics
Coloured markers for face and feet
Fusible web: Bondaweb or similar
Glue stick or other craft glue
Sequins, beads, lace, cord or other
  decorations for trees

EQUIPMENT
Basic sewing kit (needles, pins, scissors,
  tacking thread, etc)
Template plastic
Soapstone or chalk pencil
Black marker pen

Note: Instructions are for fusible appliqué. For hand appliqué, add ¼ in (6 mm) for turnings all round.

PREPARING THE FABRIC

1   To make the circle, fold the background fabric in half and then in half again, into quarters. Make an arc 24 in (61 cm) from the corner: a pin with a piece of string tied to it, and a pencil tied to the other end will make an accurate curve; or swing a ruler with a pencil or marker. Cut along the line you have marked.

2   On the background circle, cut from the outer edge to the centre for the opening.

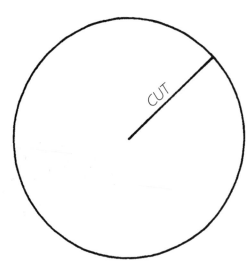

3   Make plastic templates, tracing them from the template diagrams. (Add ¼ in (6 mm) all round for turnings if using hand appliqué.)

FATHER CHRISTMASES

4   From flesh-coloured fabric cut:
12 x template 3a
24 x template 7 (allow the extra ¼ in (6 mm) only on the straight edge)

5   From red fabric cut:
6 x template 1
6 x template 4
6 x template 5
6 x template 6

6   From green fabric cut:
6 x template 1
6 x template 4
6 x template 5
6 x template 6

7   From white fabric cut:
12 x template 2
12 x template 3

8   Referring to the photograph, and the diagram on page 130, use fusible web to fuse piece 3a on top of piece 3.

9   Make six red and six green Father Christmases, piecing (sewing) them together, very carefully, in numerical order. Finish them by fusing on the hands, tucking the extra ¼ in (6 mm) over the outer edge. Draw the noses, eyes and mouths with fabric pens and add eyebrows and moustaches in white cotton.

FATHER CHRISTMAS TEMPLATES: Actual size

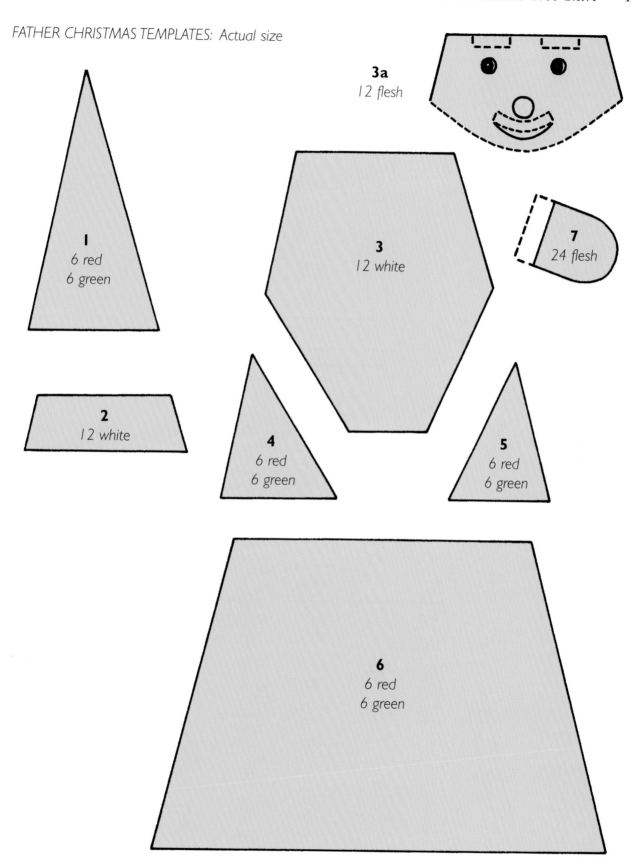

3a
12 flesh

1
6 red
6 green

3
12 white

7
24 flesh

2
12 white

4
6 red
6 green

5
6 red
6 green

6
6 red
6 green

FATHER CHRISTMAS DIAGRAM:
85% actual size

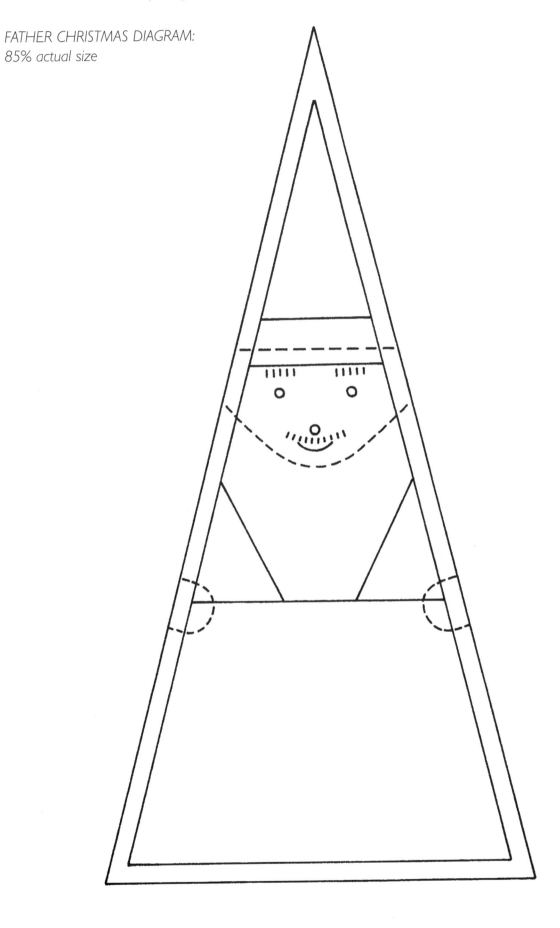

OTHER SHAPES

10 Cut 24 teardrop balls.

Cut 24 trees.

Cut 12 outer border pieces (see page 132) from same fabric as teardrops.

Cut 24 trunk pieces from brown scraps.

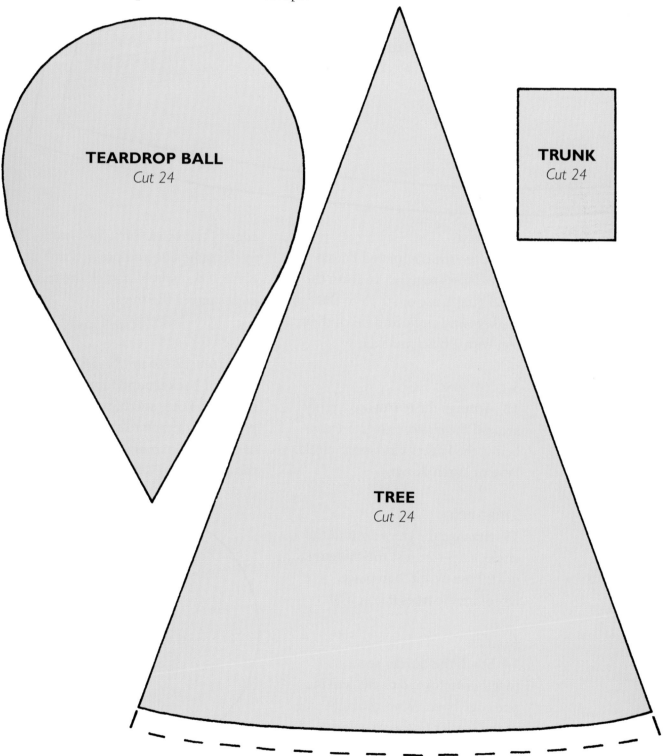

TEARDROP BALL
Cut 24

TRUNK
Cut 24

TREE
Cut 24

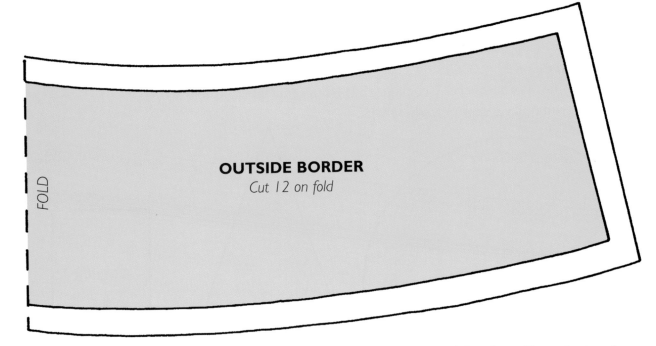

OUTSIDE BORDER
Cut 12 on fold

FOLD

FIRST RING

11 Stitch the completed Father Christmases together to form the inner ring. Fuse or stitch to the background circle and mark their feet with a black marker.

SECOND RING

12 Arrange the teardrops evenly around the circle, 1 in (2.5 cm) below the Father Christmas circle. Fuse or stitch down.

THIRD RING

13 Arrange the trees around the circle, each tree just touching the next. Fuse or stitch in place. Decorate the trees if you wish.

BORDER

14 Stitch the border sections together to form a circle, leaving one edge open. With the right side of the border to the wrong side of the skirt, stitch the border to the edge of the skirt. Turn the border to the right side and press. Stitch in place. Then stitch or stick the trunk pieces under the trees.

TIES

15 From 12–14 in (30–35 cm) strips of background fabric, make four ties. Fold, stitch, turn and press. Pin or tack to the right side of the skirt, two on either side of the cut.

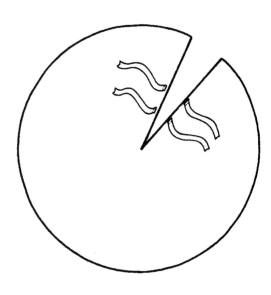

ASSEMBLY

16 Lay the right side of circle to wadding and right side of backing. Pin or tack, then stitch all round leaving an opening for turning to right side (right). Turn, press and slip-stitch the opening together.

17 Cut out a 3 in (7.5 cm) hole from the centre of the skirt, and bind it with bias tape.

18 Quilt as desired by hand or machine.

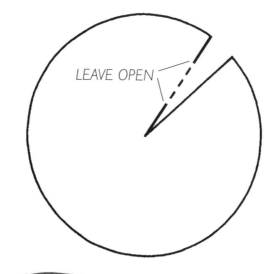

'Art Nouveau' Wall-Hanging

❖ *Barbara Furse* ❖

This charming little wall-hanging is a slightly smaller version of the design used for the trapunto and shadow-quilted cushions earlier in the book (see pages 62–70). It is worked in one of my favourite Liberty fabrics, and would make an elegant addition to any bedroom's decor.

MATERIALS

2 x 18 in (46 cm) squares black cotton, for background and backing

18 in (46 cm) square wadding

Four 2 x 19 in (5 x 48.5 cm) pieces black cotton for edging

Small pieces coloured fabrics for patches

Quilting thread

Black sewing thread

EQUIPMENT

Basic sewing kit (needles, pins, scissors, tacking thread, etc)

Template plastic

Soapstone or chalk pencil

1 Find the centre of the fabric square as described in Basic Technique, page 17. Mark a circle with an 6½ in (17 cm) radius, to help with placement of patches.

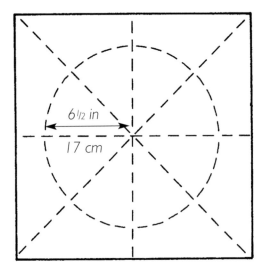

2 Make plastic templates, tracing them from the template diagram on page 66. Cut the shapes from the patterned fabrics, adding ¼ in (6 mm) all round for turnings.

3 Make up the shapes (see page 19), arrange them on the background (opposite), and stitch in place. Press.

4 Make the quilting 'sandwich' (see Quilting, page 24) and quilt around each patch.

5 Edge the square as follows: fold strips in half lengthways, press. Put raw edges together on raw edge of the square on right side. Stitch ¼ in (6 mm) along edge through all layers. Turn over strip to the back, slip stitch in place, mitring the corners.

6 Attach a small sleeve at the back for hanging (see Hanging a Quilt, page 30).

TIP
Choosing fabrics
Most of the pieces in this book could be made using scraps of coloured fabric, except for the backgrounds. But it's much more fun to buy new fabric.

About the Author

ANGELA BESLEY has been sewing since she was six years old, and has been a quilter for about fifteen years.

She teaches workshops on various forms of quilting, and has demonstrated her rose-window techniques at quilt fairs for several years.

Angela lives in Buckinghamshire, England, with her very supportive and encouraging husband, and her Neapolitan alley cat, Emma, who firmly believes that all quilts are made for her benefit.

Angela's daughter, Gail Lawther, is a well-known quilter, embroiderer and published author.

INDEX

Project titles are given in italics.
Page numbers marked *t* refer to Tip Boxes.

TITLES AVAILABLE FROM
GMC Publications
BOOKS

WOODCARVING

Beginning Woodcarving — GMC Publications
Carving Architectural Detail in Wood: The Classical Tradition — Frederick Wilbur
Carving Birds & Beasts — GMC Publications
Carving the Human Figure: Studies in Wood and Stone — Dick Onians
Carving Nature: Wildlife Studies in Wood — Frank Fox-Wilson
Carving on Turning — Chris Pye
Decorative Woodcarving — Jeremy Williams
Elements of Woodcarving — Chris Pye
Essential Woodcarving Techniques — Dick Onians
Lettercarving in Wood: A Practical Course — Chris Pye
Making & Using Working Drawings for Realistic Model Animals — Basil F. Fordham
Power Tools for Woodcarving — David Tippey
Relief Carving in Wood: A Practical Introduction — Chris Pye
Understanding Woodcarving in the Round — GMC Publications
Useful Techniques for Woodcarvers — GMC Publications
Woodcarving: A Foundation Course — Zoë Gertner
Woodcarving for Beginners — GMC Publications
Woodcarving Tools, Materials & Equipment (New Edition) — Chris Pye

WOODTURNING

Adventures in Woodturning — David Springett
Bert Marsh: Woodturner — Bert Marsh
Bowl Turning Techniques Masterclass — Tony Boase
Colouring Techniques for Woodturners — Jan Sanders
Contemporary Turned Wood: New Perspectives in a Rich Tradition — Ray Leier, Jan Peters & Kevin Wallace
The Craftsman Woodturner — Peter Child
Decorating Turned Wood: The Maker's Eye — Liz & Michael O'Donnell
Decorative Techniques for Woodturners — Hilary Bowen
Illustrated Woodturning Techniques — John Hunnex
Intermediate Woodturning Projects — GMC Publications
Keith Rowley's Woodturning Projects — Keith Rowley
Making Screw Threads in Wood — Fred Holder
Turned Boxes: 50 Designs — Chris Stott
Turning Green Wood — Michael O'Donnell
Turning Pens and Pencils — Kip Christensen & Rex Burningham
Useful Woodturning Projects — GMC Publications
Woodturning: Bowls, Platters, Hollow Forms, Vases, Vessels, Bottles, Flasks, Tankards, Plates — GMC Publications
Woodturning: A Foundation Course (New Edition) — Keith Rowley
Woodturning: A Fresh Approach — Robert Chapman
Woodturning: An Individual Approach — Dave Regester
Woodturning: A Source Book of Shapes — John Hunnex
Woodturning Jewellery — Hilary Bowen

Woodturning Masterclass — Tony Boase
Woodturning Techniques — GMC Publications

WOODWORKING

Advanced Scrollsaw Projects — GMC Publications
Beginning Picture Marquetry — Lawrence Threadgold
Bird Boxes and Feeders for the Garden — Dave Mackenzie
Complete Woodfinishing — Ian Hosker
David Charlesworth's Furniture-Making Techniques — David Charlesworth
David Charlesworth's Furniture-Making Techniques – Volume 2 — David Charlesworth
The Encyclopedia of Joint Making — Terrie Noll
Furniture-Making Projects for the Wood Craftsman — GMC Publications
Furniture-Making Techniques for the Wood Craftsman — GMC Publications
Furniture Restoration (Practical Crafts) — Kevin Jan Bonner
Furniture Restoration: A Professional at Work — John Lloyd
Furniture Restoration and Repair for Beginners — Kevin Jan Bonner
Furniture Restoration Workshop — Kevin Jan Bonner
Green Woodwork — Mike Abbott
Intarsia: 30 Patterns for the Scrollsaw — John Everett
Kevin Ley's Furniture Projects — Kevin Ley
Making Chairs and Tables — GMC Publications
Making Chairs and Tables – Volume 2 — GMC Publications
Making Classic English Furniture — Paul Richardson
Making Heirloom Boxes — Peter Lloyd
Making Little Boxes from Wood — John Bennett
Making Screw Threads in Wood — Fred Holder
Making Shaker Furniture — Barry Jackson
Making Woodwork Aids and Devices — Robert Wearing
Mastering the Router — Ron Fox
Pine Furniture Projects for the Home — Dave Mackenzie
Practical Scrollsaw Patterns — John Everett
Router Magic: Jigs, Fixtures and Tricks to Unleash your Router's Full Potential — Bill Hylton
Router Tips & Techniques — Robert Wearing
Routing: A Workshop Handbook — Anthony Bailey
Routing for Beginners — Anthony Bailey
Sharpening: The Complete Guide — Jim Kingshott
Sharpening Pocket Reference Book — Jim Kingshott
Simple Scrollsaw Projects — GMC Publications
Space-Saving Furniture Projects — Dave Mackenzie
Stickmaking: A Complete Course — Andrew Jones & Clive George
Stickmaking Handbook — Andrew Jones & Clive George
Storage Projects for the Router — GMC Publications
Test Reports: The Router and Furniture & Cabinetmaking — GMC Publications
Veneering: A Complete Course — Ian Hosker

GARDENING

Auriculas for Everyone: How to Grow and Show Perfect Plants

Mary Robinson

Beginners' Guide to Herb Gardening   *Yvonne Cuthbertson*

Bird Boxes and Feeders for the Garden   *Dave Mackenzie*

The Birdwatcher's Garden   *Hazel & Pamela Johnson*

Broad-Leaved Evergreens   *Stephen G. Haw*

Companions to Clematis: Growing Clematis with Other Plants

Marigold Badcock

Creating Contrast with Dark Plants   *Freya Martin*

Creating Small Habitats for Wildlife in your Garden   *Josie Briggs*

Exotics are Easy   *GMC Publications*

Gardening with Wild Plants   *Julian Slatcher*

Growing Cacti and Other Succulents in the Conservatory and Indoors

Shirley-Anne Bell

Growing Cacti and Other Succulents in the Garden   *Shirley-Anne Bell*

Hardy Perennials: A Beginner's Guide   *Eric Sawford*

Hedges: Creating Screens and Edges   *Averil Bedrich*

The Living Tropical Greenhouse: Creating a Haven for Butterflies

John & Maureen Tampion

Orchids are Easy: A Beginner's Guide to their Care and Cultivation

Tom Gilland

Plant Alert: A Garden Guide for Parents   *Catherine Collins*

Planting Plans for Your Garden   *Jenny Shukman*

Plants that Span the Seasons   *Roger Wilson*

Sink and Container Gardening Using Dwarf Hardy Plants

Chris & Valerie Wheeler

The Successful Conservatory and Growing Exotic Plants   *Joan Phelan*

VIDEOS

Drop-in and Pinstuffed Seats   *David James*

Stuffover Upholstery   *David James*

Elliptical Turning   *David Springett*

Woodturning Wizardry   *David Springett*

Turning Between Centres: The Basics   *Dennis White*

Turning Bowls   *Dennis White*

Boxes, Goblets and Screw Threads   *Dennis White*

Novelties and Projects   *Dennis White*

Classic Profiles   *Dennis White*

Twists and Advanced Turning   *Dennis White*

Sharpening the Professional Way   *Jim Kingshott*

Sharpening Turning & Carving Tools   *Jim Kingshott*

Bowl Turning   *John Jordan*

Hollow Turning   *John Jordan*

Woodturning: A Foundation Course   *Keith Rowley*

Carving a Figure: The Female Form   *Ray Gonzalez*

The Router: A Beginner's Guide   *Alan Goodsell*

The Scroll Saw: A Beginner's Guide   *John Burke*

MAGAZINES

WOODTURNING ✦ WOODCARVING
WOODWORKING ✦ THE ROUTER
FURNITURE & CABINETMAKING
THE DOLLS' HOUSE MAGAZINE
MACHINE KNITTING NEWS
OUTDOOR PHOTOGRAPHY
BLACK & WHITE PHOTOGRAPHY
BUSINESSMATTERS

The above represents a full list of the titles currently published or scheduled to be published.
All are available direct from the Publishers or through bookshops, newsagents and specialist retailers.
To place an order, or to obtain a complete catalogue, contact:

GMC Publications,
Castle Place, 166 High Street, Lewes, East Sussex BN7 1XU United Kingdom
Tel: 01273 488005 Fax: 01273 478606
E-mail: pubs@thegmcgroup.com

Orders by credit card are accepted